UNSPOKEN
LINGUISTICS

COMMUNICATION STRATEGY AND DEFENSE

Stephanie Y. Arteaga

PROISLE PUBLISHING

© COPYRIGHT 2024 BY STEPHANIE Y. ARTEAGA

ISBN: 978-1-965498-07-1

All rights reserved. No part of this book may be reproduced or transmitted in any form or by any means, electronic or mechanical, including photocopying, recording, or by any information storage and retrieval system, without permission in writing from the copyright owner.

The views expressed in this work are solely those of the author and do not necessarily reflect the views of the publisher, and the publisher disclaims any responsibility for them.

To order additional copies of this book, contact:

Proisle Publishing Services LLC
39-67 58th Street, 1st floor
Woodside, NY 11377, USA
Phone: (+1 646-480-0129)
info@proislepublishing.com

Table of Contents

- CHAPTER ONE — 1
- CHAPTER TWO — 9
- CHAPTER THREE — 19
- CHAPTER FOUR — 23
- CHAPTER FIVE — 31
- CHAPTER SIX — 37
- CHAPTER SEVEN — 47
- CHAPTER EIGHT — 51
- CHAPTER NINE — 55
- CHAPTER TEN — 59
- CHAPTER ELEVEN — 63
- CHAPTER TWELVE — 73
- CHAPTER THIRTEEN — 83
- CHAPTER FOURTEEN — 95
- CHAPTER FIFTEEN — 105
- CHAPTER SIXTEEN — 113
- CHAPTER SEVENTEEN — 123
- CHAPTER EIGHTEEN — 133
- CHAPTER NINETEEN — 143

CHAPTER ONE

I've just discovered the "American" mentality: 'Do whatever it takes, no matter what anyone else thinks, to make a living!' This amazing realization came to me while watching a television talk show this morning. My situation is destitute. There isn't much food, all of our bills are overdue and no work. I don't know why I'm in this situation. I guess I'm just useless. I can't keep a job. I didn't ask for much and can't understand why everything is so hopeless.

When I was younger, I only focused on the romantic side of career choices. I didn't give much thought to financial security and choosing a job to support myself and family. I just loved thinking about the prestige that I would have with 'dream' professions. I believed that my profession in itself was supposed to make me well thought of and respected. It was supposed to define my greatness. Now I believe that one should just choose a job that pays the bills!

Lately, I've been inwardly critical of others so I decided to try a new strategy in listening. I have begun to study *how* others communicate, not the content or context of what they say. The guest, female, she was who inspired my thesis statement was on the 'witness stand' in defense of her maternal ethics. She had a habit of prefacing each response to the attacks and inquiries with the phrase, "But you know what...?" I suddenly realized that this was a trained response and I was certain that she had actually paid someone to teach her communication strategy. It was a stall technique, true enough, but it didn't come off as a hostile counter attack. I'm sure the other viewers would agree with my summation of her character as being one of strength, clarity and confidence. Another male guest chose to number his thoughts as in "first of all..., secondly..., three... etc.

I could discern that this was a very clear-thinking and organized person. Then I heard a female speaker often interject a "yes" between her statements. This technique provided affirmation and made her opinions seem valid. Finally, the talk show host, female she was, used a diplomatic adjective, "interesting" to respond to the subjects on which she needed to remain neutral. She also used a psychological bridge, "What does that mean...?" to prompt a guest to expand upon an idea or thought. I've heard psychiatrists and psychologists use the same strategy when they say, "Tell me more". I now realize that I haven't been giving the producers and players of these types of programs sufficient credit for their efforts.

Now, allow me to go to the more skeptical review of the morning show. I don't understand the expression, "If he were a real man..." or "If she were a real woman..." What that says to me is that the speaker is competing; daring the subject to be as great as he or she is (or as great as they believe that they are). I can only see the referenced statement as an attack, raw and pompous. I would not call it confident. Is this a bully? It is difficult to believe that a person that repeatedly uses this expression has suffered through the chastisement that one has to endure to achieve an acceptable system of self-discipline. I don't want to break anyone's spirit or make them feel worthless. I simply am afraid of insulting others because, in my experience, they always come back – even more powerful. I do get angry. However, even then I know that there will be a penalty for my outbursts. You see, I pay for and suffer for what I say; even for what I allow others to say in my presence. There is something that inhabits me that is overly sensitive to the impact of idle words. Perhaps this person is not a bully; however, bullies are often known to goad others into doing things that they are not comfortable in doing.

Here's something else: I don't understand why I am offended when people, especially educated people, use words or phrases that I don't use. Should I feel cheated, stupid or impressed? Perhaps, I'm jealous of them for doing well when I'm not. I'm jealous of other people having their lives together when mine is falling apart. But maybe now things won't seem strange when people say things that I've been afraid to say. Is it possible that this all started when someone told me that everyone would suffer if I didn't do my job? Those same people thought nothing of seeing me fired. You see, we all didn't go down. It was just ME. It was just me who took the blame when everything wrong happened.

Here I am, ironically, just getting inspiration to actually write a book when my car note and rent are seriously overdue. Being without work has taken the control away but really may be the antidote that I need to write. I find it difficult to write but I have discovered that I MUST write in order to remain calm, to release inward agony, to reorganize my confused thoughts and to defend myself and others. This is not a story book. It is an analysis. I have to restore my perspective to a healthy status. I want to believe that I can return to enjoying my life again. For example: I have learned, just today, to make my responses relevant to the person to whom I am speaking. Maybe if I gather enough communication tips and strategies, I will actually be able to say something worthwhile in the pages to come.

There are many reasons that come to my mind that I have not completed a book before now. They could be perceived as excuses so I will just be grateful that I plan to completely write this one. I have been secretly hoping that someone else would be so taken with my person that they would be inspired to write a book in my honor. Wishful thinking. I must be the one to write from my own perspective. Most of the books that I have read have been written when the authors have arrived at the point of success and have decided to recount the road to success. I don't know why my inspiration has come when I am at such a low point in my life and writing seems to be, not a way out, but just something to do.

Not very long ago, I saw a worker dressed as a slice of pizza dancing on the sidewalk. I believe that he or she must have had some inhibitions about taking on such a task when there are so many more glamorous dancing and acting jobs in the market. But that is just another example of the 'American' mindset. A little bit of humility is well worth having enough money for food, shelter, transportation and definitely leisure expenses. That humility does not compare to the humiliation of creditor collection calls, court appearances for eviction and a tow truck showing up to repossess one's vehicle when the neighbors are watching. The sidewalk dancer could certainly justify writing a road-to-success story more so than I can. There cannot be a road to success when there is no success. That worker has succeeded at having something that I do not have: A job!

Now that my jobless state has been established, I do not choose to write about how I arrived at this point. I will simply write about my perspective. If others should choose to read what I have written, they can draw their own conclusions.

Even now that I proclaim to know the 'American' focus, there continues to be another missing element that I've known about but never possessed. It seems to be a key ingredient that human resource agents look for and top executives promote. The Russian elite call it "wit". The English call it "clever". I call it "brown-nosing". I have never even come close to being able to fake this 'job-nabbing', 'get-a-better-course-grade' strategy. I just cannot maneuver hints of persuasion to get management to hire me! Now let me go to the 'Thesis Lady' statement, "But you know what…?" I do pretty well at selling other people or 'going to bat for' others. The unfortunate thing is that I have not been able to make a living doing this, neither written or verbally. When I am writing, I feel as though it is what I need to do. But thinking practically, I have nothing to convince a local newspaper to give me a job as a writer.

What I have noticed is that not only are family businesses passed down from generation to generation, but occupations are also reserved for legacy holders. The office of admissions at universities and colleges is very keen on sifting through enrollment applications looking for children of professionals and their colleagues. This process becomes even more precise at the graduate levels. If someone from the outer circle is able to make the grades to certify a profession, the battle is only one-half of the way won.

Nepotism is like the pitcher for the New York Yankees. It will strike you out almost every time! After all, we do not want just anyone touching or examining our unclothed bodies in the medical examination room. We do not wish to reveal our innermost secrets to strangers during psychiatric therapy. We do not want lawyers, whose families have a social status that may negatively influence a borderline judgment, representing us or our love ones. These thoughts, both valid and vital were never clearly put to me when I left for the university. There was only one subtle note of what was to come. During my first summer break from classes, I was speaking to someone about my plans to become a medical examiner. His response took me by surprise; "Isn't that political?" he asked. I thought to myself, *'Surely, they don't have to vote me into a position to look at dead bodies all day!'* Do you see the illusion of glamour that I spoke of earlier beginning to appear now? I thought only of being brave enough to take on such a task. Jack Klugman of television's 'Quincy' made this profession look so very appealing. But I, supposedly possessing an above-average aptitude score, did not see the occupation for what it really is. Of course, all jobs have new facets that arise daily. But I am indeed embarrassed to say that I had no clue of the true meaning or impact of the question, "Isn't that political?"

I did not realize that dead bodies are equally as important as live bodies. One key factor is that they always tell a story that reveals that something went wrong.

CHAPTER TWO

Irony seems to frequently show up in my life. Each time that I go to recite my residence address, ### Cemetery Road, there is always this pause. At first, it was comical, a conversation piece even. But lately, it has kept the question of death ever present.

I received court eviction papers today. Reality has finally surfaced! Well, at least things are more absolute in my mind now. Perhaps my perception of justice will be restored through this ordeal as well. It is more frightening to wait for something bad to happen than when it happens (or maybe I just have not experienced enough real tragedy to know what frightening really is). I do not know if the Department of Human Services will assist with past-due rent but I am feeling better that they have been officially notified.

I did not feel the anger that I have felt today during my walk to the cemetery. I have never had an understanding of death. The apartment is very quiet since digital broadcast began today and there is no money to pay for cable television or a digital television set. I had 650 new messages in my America online mailbox! I managed to quickly scan and delete all but 20 in my thirty-minute allotment at the library's personal computer. The public library building was transformed from a funeral home. It is very comfortable in spite of the fact that it was formerly used to temporarily house the dead.

My theory of death is that the consciousness of a deceased person goes into a dream state at the time of death. Each time we sleep, it is a rehearsal of death. I have heard it said that extinct dinosaurs never came out of hibernation. They never woke from their sleep. I see death as being something similar to hibernation. The spirit may fly through dream land until a new physical home is found for it. It is possible that meeting death and succumbing to it is like trusting a swim instructor to not let you drown. I have never learned to swim.

Unexplained and sudden death is unnerving. I speculate that we do not get the entire story most times. The surviving family members certainly would not welcome hints of fault cast upon the fallen beloved during their time of grief. I, too, believe in the cautious saying that prohibits one from speaking ill of the dead. It is taboo even for some of the most brutal personalities. It is difficult to perceive that the same ruthlessness that allows someone to cut another's throat or to scalp another can be housed in the same psyche of a person capable of bonified tears of grief.

Because of the lack of money, I have been buying meat very sparingly. A few weeks ago, I purchased a ten-pound bag of chicken leg quarters, planning to ration the pieces to last throughout the week. I opened the bag and began to separate the lot into smaller portions and re-bagging them into small storage bags. When I got to the bottom of the bag, there was something that shook me very deeply. It was a tiny hen, complete except for its head. What was sickening is that when I looked at it, it closely resembled the body of a newborn HUMAN infant missing its head, hands and feet. I quickly placed it in a separate bag and threw it into the freezer for fear of going into a psychosis. A mental breakdown just cannot be tolerated! I have worked with some very severely handicapped and deformed youth. One student only showed up with a head and torso or trunk –no legs and arms. But the remarkable fact is that those children helped my humanity to remain intact. I felt human. The tiny hen, however, shattered my humanity for an instant. I am afraid of eating another being like myself.

Since that time, I have felt the lack of food is convenient. The thought of what others have to do to satisfy hunger conveniently eludes us most often.

I am comfortable in believing in the intelligence of life forms outside of the human race. The tiny ant has a well-structured society. I imagine that domestic farm animals grieve for the loss of their young. Surely they are able to sense when they are about to be slaughtered and fear the nearing assassination. Even a giant Clydesdale must enjoy a rest from toting carts and riders when it is allowed. Steers can often be seen trying to find shelter in an open graze space when the threat of rain is signaled from the clouds in the sky. There is an air of acceptance in the midst of sheep lined up to be sheared. Even frogs will suddenly make a large splash to frighten trespassers away from their domain. Wolves bay at the moon. Canines shed tears. Raccoons fight and felines can balance themselves on fence rails as perfectly as the finest gymnast! When I perceive my surroundings in this fashion, there is rest for my anguished spirit.

Tiny human hands in motion are amazing to watch. It is refreshing to see an infant establish the extension of his or her own will when they begin to reach out and grab for objects. They are fascinated by the abilities that we often forget to appreciate. I believe that there is a way of maintaining this zeal for achievement so that they have a thirst for it at school age. It is true that nearly 100% of children are excited to begin school. But for some, it dissipates before they even finish kindergarten! Something is tearing away the excitement and eagerness from these little ones.

Could it be bullies that are attacking these children? Could it be that they are missing the home environment? I do not believe that the latter is true because the faltering economy does not allow most mothers to remain home all day, coddling their children until they reach school age. There must be bullies in the school! They are not the traditional "over-sized" kids that terrorize others on the playground. Forced teaching is likely the culprit.

Believe it or not, most children already have an established learning style by the age of five. When that style does not correspond to the uniformity that greets them in the classroom environment, their young minds go into a panic!! The manifestations of this panic can be as individually unique as the snowflakes that fall from the winter sky. Some will be openly hostile and defiant. Some will be passive-aggressive, deciding to show the teacher that they are in charge, leading the other pupils in gags and folly. Some will weep. Some will whine. Some will become almost catatonic, refusing to speak or communicate in any way. Some will wet their pants just so that their mothers will come rescue them. There are many, many ways that they will express their frustration but they almost never admit that they do not understand. In fact, when questioned about their understanding, they would rather deny it than suffer the threat of ridicule or discipline for not being able to understand! We must find some way to rescue these suffering children.

Unfortunately, the social hierarchy is already in place at this stage as well. Teachers are often forced to cater to the whims of the children whose parents 'own the town'. These children sometimes get a private school education at the expense of the poorer that have to be ignored while the rich child is re-organizing the classroom. Classroom control is so very vital even at this young age. Of course, small children do not seem to be a violent threat but this is a very dangerous misconception. Listen to this story:

A substitute was scheduled to come in at mid-day for the afternoon session. In order to be on time, she had to put off going to the restroom. The regular instructor greeted her with hurried notes and expectations. There was only five minutes before the students had to be called in from the playground. Trying to be as tactful as possible, the substitute blurted that she needed to be excused to go to the restroom. Although the instructor was annoyed that she could not leave at that point, she had no choice but to relent and go to the back door to greet the students while the substitute took her leave. The substitute did not tarry and quickly emerged from the restroom, dashing to the back entrance where the students were already beginning to file into the classroom. This was not an agreeable set up for the substitute since one of her most effective strategies was to quickly memorize the names of her students. But she carefully recited back each name as she gathered them from the murmurs and jibber of the small students. As the regular instructor exited she quickly and discretely whispered to the substitute, "Keep an eye on Ruby!" Not very clear on what this meant, the substitute nodded her agreement and scanned the classroom for the child's location. At the moment, she was not causing mischief but had established an aloof and mysterious demeanor. The substitute only hesitated for an instant before delving into the lesson plans laid out before her. Shortly into the lesson, an official appeared at the doorway and announced that she needed to take a few of the students with her for a brief consultation. The substitute nodded in submission to the official's request but continued with the lesson as the selected students, 'Ruby' being one of the chosen, filed out of the classroom. The substitute was busy with the lesson plan when the recessed students returned, but in a sideways glance, she noticed that Ruby had re-entered, almost in flight and looked to be hiding something. Looking closely, the substitute spied a tiny object that glimmered like glass in the child's mouth. The substitute quickly and cautiously approached the child trying to get a closer look without alarming the child as she herself was alarmed. The child backed away in defiance, "MY candy!" Still not quite able to see what the object was but knowing that this was urgent, the substitute instinctively reached out to snatch the object from the child's mouth. The child dashedly turned her head away and the removal attempt failed.

Thankfully, the substitute could still see the glimmer, confirming that the child had not yet swallowed the glass-looking object. The child, Ruby, now knew that she held the attention and control of the entire class and took advantage of the opportunity to poke her tongue out holding the object and then snatching it back in to tease the substitute.

"MY candy!" she announced, maintaining adamant defiance. The substitute grasped the opportunities that the child gave her to catch glimpses of the object still with no success in determining what it was. She decided that she would have to be humble,

"I don't think that's candy. May I see your candy?" The child considered this for a moment, cautiously dragging her tongue out for only an instant longer than before. Having still no idea what it was, the substitute called on the other students for their opinions,

"Do you think it's candy?"

"No, I don't think that's candy!" each chimed in turn. Prompted by the consensus of disbelief, Ruby held out her tongue even longer but quickly pulled it back before it could be taken or identified. Still, the substitute persisted,

"I have candy, Ruby. It's not like your candy. My candy is sweet and tasty. I have very sweet candy." She walked over to her tote bag and pulling out a small box of mints, she flashed the container before the child's eyes. It worked! This distraction prompted the child to remove the object from her mouth and reach for the mints. Seizing the opportunity, the substitute quickly grabbed the object with the opposite hand with which she held the box of mints. Recognizing that the danger had not passed because the child could easily replace the other object with something else harmful, she took the opportunity to try to convince the child once and for all that she could not continue with this type of behavior. The substitute held up both hands, each containing one of the objects. Nodding at the hand with the mints, she sang,

"Oh, my candy is so-o sweet!" But shifting her glance to the other hand, she said, "If you swallow this, it will go into your stomach and make it hurt really bad! – Like this!" she punched herself in the stomach.

"Like this!" she punched again.

The children giggled. Ruby, who seemed really pleased to see the substitute inflict pain on herself but still not convinced of the trade-off, reached for the mints again. The substitute did not want to introduce sweets into the child's diet without proper consent so she handed over the box stipulating,

"You may hold my candy for me but DO NOT OPEN THE BOX!"

The child was the envy of all of her classmates and they all crowded around her to peer into the mint box. It was not long before she was prodded into opening the lid and dividing the candy. The substitute called this to a halt, instructing Ruby to collect all of the pieces and return them to the box.

The object, which turned out to be a piece of plastic, was recovered. Despite it not being glass, the substitute was thankful for the removal of the potential choke hazard.

In reviewing the story, I find that the success of the recovery overshadows a disturbing detail. The child was a danger to herself and to those around her. The lesson was completely abandoned during the rescue that everyone else had to audience. The substitute having no choice in this life-threatening situation rewarded a child for misconduct. This is a KINDERGARTEN setting! What trend do you see established from this incident? Where were the control devices that should have been in place before the child's behavior escalated to this point? The substitute was only present for that day but what about the children who have to continue in that setting?

...There is no joy in Muddville today.

CHAPTER THREE

Speaking in the child Ruby's defense, I will briefly touch upon what may have been her problem on that particular day. This does not excuse or explain away all of what went on with the substitute. In examining her actions, I find them very devious and WELL rehearsed for a child of her age.

Continuing with the substitute's visit, not long after the children reassembled for the lesson, the time arrived for physical education. They were escorted by the substitute to the gymnasium. The substitute had been doting on the child Ruby since the earlier incident, sensing that the child must have been desperate for something to act out in such a way. She was sure that something had seriously angered this child. For one, she was bilingual and the substitute conversed with the child Ruby in Spanish. This seemed to warm the child to her. So inwardly traumatized but not wanting to lose this newfound alliance, the substitute would have done most anything to please the child. She allowed the child Ruby to come to the front of the line and clasped her smaller hand with her own as they led the group to the gymnasium. The substitute, with her imperfect Spanish, spoke to the child on the way to the gymnasium. This was to be a happy day for the substitute – she had made a friend! When they arrived at the gymnasium entrance, the physical education instructor took over, separating the children for the planned activities. She did something, however, that prompted the substitute to stay and observe. The child Ruby and another female student were removed from the play area and told to watch from the sidelines in front of the gymnasium wall. Not feeling that it was her place to interfere but not wanting to destroy child Ruby's confidence in her, the substitute discretely tip-toed over to the child and speaking in Spanish, asked the child what had happened. The physical education instructor, sensing what the conversation was about, walked over and re-explained to both the substitute and the child Ruby that the child Ruby's shoes could not be worn on the floor of the gymnasium because they would scrape the finish. Thinking that the child did not understand enough English, the substitute attempted to translate but faltered making it apparent to the physical education instructor that she was very amateur in her skills. In response, the physical education instructor repeated the play requirement. The substitute realized that in trying to be the child Ruby's ally, she had let everyone else down. Embarrassed and hurt, she promised the child Ruby that she would return promptly and exited the gymnasium.

Now, one has to wonder; what was the real problem? The substitute showed great skill and intellect when alone with the children, but it appears that the child Ruby's acceptance was only feigned and for a selfish purpose at that. She wanted the substitute to go to battle with the physical education instructor when she, herself, already understood the rules. Apparently, her parents could not afford to buy her the shoes that she needed for physical education and she thought that if the substitute and the physical education instructor fought, she would have her revenge for being denied her way. THIS child understood the classroom set up perfectly! She knew that the substitute was vulnerable, with the lack of confidence from not being a native Spanish speaker and not having a teaching degree. She played on that vulnerability to humiliate the substitute. Again, this child is dangerous!

Children like the child Ruby do not seem to be a threat when an individual is in their presence. In fact, they can make victims feel very heroic and very much needed. We do not understand their capabilities... All we can really do is submit to what seems right at the time and act upon it.

A caregiver for this child had better have their wits about them and always remain guarded. The mental anguish that can be inflicted by an episode like the one just disclosed, can be devastating. Imagine if the recovery, if it was even necessary since the child is supposed to be such a great actress and all, had not been a success and the child had choked and perished. Most likely the child would have been hailed a saint and the substitute would have lost all merit and credibility. The child's behavior prior to this hypothetical demise would have gone completely unaddressed and completely ignored as an explanation of what caused her hypothetical end. Again, we can only submit to what seems right at the time and act upon it. Suppositions of what might have happened only entice an undesired fear. We have to keep our focus on the behavior.

CHAPTER FOUR

Finally, the last item that needs to be mentioned about the day with the child Ruby:

The substitute received a note instructing her to send several pieces of information home with the children. In the rush of the departure, one piece of the child Ruby's information was left behind. However, discovering it before the transportation vehicles had left the school grounds, the substitute ran out to the loading area in search of the child. There were many children lined up, ready to embark. The substitute desperately searched for the child Ruby. Not catching sight of the child, she urgently called,

"Has anyone seen Ruby? Doesn't she ride this bus?"

A student behind her spoke up, "Yeah! She rides the same bus that I do!"

The substitute was thankful and requested, "I forgot to give her something. Will you make sure that she gets it?"

The student volunteer agreed, taking the paper in hand. The substitute reeled back in relief. This had been a most memorable encounter!

I finally answered one of the numerous auto finance collection calls. They plan to submit my file for repossession review if I don't send them at least one payment within the next day or two. I do not know if it would be prudent to request another extension on my auto loan but I do know that this is not a good time to lose the use of the vehicle. Prior to this time, I avoided these telephone calls but something finally gave me the resolve to grasp the telephone receiver and speak. I was on my daily walk to the cemetery and suddenly an obligatory dare was pushed into my head. I must survey the names on the headstones. Nervously, but bravely I scanned them, not quite sure of what I would find. I did not find a stone with my name on it. What I did find, however, was a small grave stone towards the peak center of the cemetery. It was simply marked, RUBY M 1883-1970. I believe the child Ruby's surname was "Moreno".

Although some indeed fascinating information has been discussed thus far, we cannot question life and death. It is quiet now and I should take advantage of the time to sleep.

The Father's Day celebration is just about one week away. I feel that it is necessary to keep up with my writing in order to not lose my edge in the midst of my financial problems. I have this depressing feeling that I am in pursuit of death. This is strange because I have not been looking for it. On the contrary, I could probably find many more appealing things to do with my time. Death is trying to capture me, I am very sure of it. Maybe I ought not make too much trouble in the cemetery since there is no reason that I could not become a resident there.

I have already stated that I thought it very unwise to speak ill will against the deceased. But what does one do when he or she is called upon to make judgment on the prior-to-death actions of the dead as their civic duty? Listen to another story:

A female citizen received a letter from the county court with a mandatory order for a jury selection appearance. She had misgivings about making judgment but since it was a legal obligation, she took great care in promptly responding to the court summons. Her fear that it may not arrive on time or get lost, urged her to pay extra postage for a return certified postcard to be sent to confirm delivery and give evidence of the response if needed. Well, the delivery of her response was successful, however, she arrived the very last of those summoned. The court officials that ushered her in did not scold her for her tardiness but some of the others that were called upon to appear, were annoyed and looked upon her as being without tact. The female citizen took a seat in the rear spectator section of the courtroom, assuming with such a large showing of candidates, that she would easily and quickly be eliminated.

Despite her 'slothful' arrival, her apparel was in no way the same. She wore a dark-colored linen suit for the occasion.

Soon the judge and attorneys for both sides took their places and began calling candidate jurors to the jury stand for interview questioning. Not very long into the process, to her surprise, the female citizen was called upon to take one of the places on the jury stand. Her responses to the questions were clear and concise, taking the others in the courtroom by surprise.

A family member who had lost a daughter, son-in-law and grandchildren in a tragic fire was suing the propane gas company for wrongful deaths benefits. A brief summary of what had occurred was laid out before all.

A question from the prosecution to the group of candidate jurors, "Has anyone ever suddenly lost a loved one?"

Almost instantly, the female citizen's hand went up in affirmative reply, "My three-and-a-half-year-old nephew died in a house fire in June of 1978. Even though it has been nearly thirty years, I can still vividly remember how I felt. I can't even begin to imagine losing more than one family member at the same time."

Another question went before the group, Could you make a decision on who is responsible and if applicable decide an amount in penalty or settlement for such a case?"

Again the female citizen's hand went up, "I don't believe that there is a price that can be put on human life but if I were legally obligated, I would make the decision. If the gas company is at fault, having to pay a large settlement may teach them to do a better job the next time."

The defense attorney for the gas company seized a portion of the female citizen's statement to counter-question her individually,

"You've stated that there is no price that can be placed on human life and yet you believe that if you are selected as a juror that you would be able to make a decision even to the extent of setting a dollar amount with your peer jurors?"

"I would if I were legally obligated to," answered the female citizen.

"You could?" the defense again countered more skeptically.

"Yes. I could" repeated the female citizen.

Again, the prosecution posed another question to the candidate jurors,

"Has anyone ever lost a parent, sibling or child?"

Yet again the female citizen responded, "I lost my father in 1988-err 1998 to an automobile accident."

At one point, the judge sternly rebuked the female citizen. She had made a questioning face in response to a detail in the report,

"You have a question?" demanded the judge.

"Was this the same explosion that happened on sixty-sixth street with the family that had recently relocated to the area?!" the female citizen asked incredulously, leaning forward on the bench.

"Yes!"

"I thought that happened more recently…" the female citizen muttered, thoroughly confused.

"This is my court and I will not tolerate disruption! Do you understand?" again the judge with stern rebuke.

The female citizen leaned back in humble submission, now knowing that she had talked too much and vowed that she would not volunteer any more responses.

Soon there was a brief recess. After reconvening, the female citizen was surprised that she was dismissed from the stand. She was told that she was free to leave.

Her feelings of shock and wounded pride prompted her to return to a spectator seat in the back of the courtroom. Another woman turned to her in a friendly inquiry that came out as a statement,

"You wanted to be called down, didn't you?"

The female citizen smiled in response, hoping that everyone else had made the same assumption. She exited the courtroom, feeling let down for not being selected to be in on something so monumental.

Later in the week, she heard that the jurors had decided to award the plaintiff a record settlement making county news history. Still feeling left out, she wished that she had been allowed to know more about the case.

In reviewing the story, I have a dreadful feeling that something went wrong – not just the explosion and the deaths but something beyond that... How did the plaintiff decide to spend the proceeds of the settlement? Think of this:

How many jobs were lost as a result of the settlement? Or how many people have not been able to pay for their propane gas supply due to a price hike that may have been used to offset the payout of this large sum of money? I am confident that there are more of these persons affected by the settlement than the number of company employees that were judged responsible by the panel of jurors. I am assuming that it was company employees that were judged responsible because the judgment was for the plaintiff or simply because it was one of their tanks that exploded without any negligence on the part of the company employees.

I have heard that large corporations will often file an insurance claim for liability damage or submit tax credit claims for exemption with the Internal Revenue Service when faced with a payable settlement. But let's return to that day of the jury selection and remember a comment made by the defense attorney:

"Let's not think about where the money is going to come from…"

Where else would it come from besides the sources that are listed above?

The neighbor to the right of the town home that I rent went missing. I spotted him this morning, walking and with a distressed facial expression. Now two women have just asked apartment maintenance and the police to investigate. They opened the door. I have told them that he's not in there. The two men exited with a report of his absence. He is a diabetic. It is unfortunate that others are having difficulty.

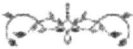

I have to buy a type-writer ribbon. I tried to unroll and sift back through the old ribbon but it didn't work. Blank. I know that I appear to be selfish to the library staff, taking up so much usage time. I'll make it a priority to buy a ribbon right away!

CHAPTER FIVE

Today's goal is to find a grave site. It is very important because its presence has made a great impact on a town's history. It marks a turning point for all who live there; a brutal murder in a small town. A beauty queen is slain in her prime for a reason that I have never known or discovered.

When I arrived at the cemetery, I parked near its very center. I went into a neighboring town to buy food today. Upon returning, I was urged to visit a different cemetery, located further away from the apartment building in which I live. Although this cemetery is smaller, it is quite a challenge to walk the rows of gravestones. I decided to make a circular path, taking great care to make sure that I did not miss what I was searching for. I had covered about eighty percent of the grounds when I, feeling that my speculation of this particular burial location was probably ill-founded, looked down and suddenly, there it was! Not more than twenty feet from where I had parked my automobile. How remarkable that I had parked so near the goal site but for some reason, had selected the opposite path direction to begin my search. Well, I am satisfied to have located it.

Thinking back to the appearance of the grave stone, it held no mention of the accomplishment of 'Bicentennial queen.' It only remarked "DAUGHTER" for its epitaph. This reminds me of the Southeast Asian burial tradition that maintains anonymity of the prior-to-death lifestyle of the deceased. Only small signs of accomplishment are noted even for the grandest of achieved merit.

Bizarre does not begin to describe the events of the night that the beauty queen died!

July 5, 1977, the headlines read: BICENTENNIAL QUEEN SLAIN. Reported subject was last seen alive leaving a night spot. It was mentioned that she left the facility alone. Her remains were found stuffed into the trunk of her vehicle. She had numerous head injuries and lacerations assumingly having suffered blows from an inflicting bare metal tire rim. Police reportedly had a suspect in custody. Three witnesses lead the police to the suspect's identity.

Soon the suspect was indicted on a murder charge and a trial began. Finally, after months of testimony, a panel of jurors submitted a 'guilty' verdict, murder one. This particular state does not include the death penalty in its bylaws; however the presiding judge for the case handed down a mandatory life sentence with no chance of parole. To date, the accused is housed in a state penitentiary.

Since then, the family of the accused has chosen to remain citizens of this same community. I often have wondered how these people have been able to remain mild and peaceful in spite of what a judged family member is experiencing. I can only imagine the pressure that they must have endured these many years.

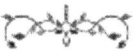

It is Saturday afternoon, just two days away from my scheduled court date. I do not have money to pay the rent and have not received word from the Department of Human Services. Well, I will just have to wait until Monday to find out if it is going to be necessary to pack. Ten days is enough time to rent a van and store away my household items. As a distraction, I decided to head for the beach to try my hand at assembling a small tent.

I decided to make a short stop at one of the shops on my way in. Not finding anything that I could use, I left. I was a little discouraged before I entered the store. I had reached the store before opening time and decided to read through my manuscript when this loud music, booming from a large white sports utility vehicle horned in on the quiet atmosphere. I endured it for as long as the owner took to do his business and leave. Then I saw someone that I have known since childhood arrive and leave in another sporty vehicle. What am I doing wrong that I cannot afford such luxury? Is an education worth nothing? Again, I just do not get it!

Believe it or not, I put the tent together and it is a small luxury, especially since it is economical, practical and quite cozy. The mesh net door is a great bonus to keep the insects out but allows me to keep abreast of what is going on outside of it. I really do like this tent.

Well, it is done! I went to court and am now free from household management responsibilities! I am looking forward to leaving all of the utilities and rent payments behind. I may lose the use of my automobile as well. A little exercise is good for me. I will have a few things to juggle but I am sure that I will be just fine. The court scene was all business.

Sad stories did not help. It was either pay the rent or leave. I am glad to concede the victory to someone who wanted to see me leave so badly. I am just not the type of clientele that they would like to have. They just do not want me there. I have tried every possible way to remain a resident but it is just not acceptable.

A BARREL OF LAUGHS

Time, time is moving in space
At a 'tick-tock' pace
White linen and lace
A ballerina dances with grace.

Time, time is moving like a jet
My thoughts, swimming with regret.
For inner pain, I need an outlet
Some inspiration, we forget.

Time, time is an expansion of one moment
What I thought I had, I no longer own it
Toss me the ball, I'll throw it
You are my friend, didn't you know it?

Who pays for laughs?
They are worth more than gold
There are so many un-trodden paths
Will they lead to riches untold?

I cannot afford laughter
That I very much need to be well
But I know if I laugh without paying what comes after
If you know where free laughs are found, do tell!

-Anonymous

CHAPTER SIX

I returned to work today. In light of my housing situation, it is a great consolation. I have been told of the death of a megastar... A spirit is in flight. Perhaps it is like the ascent and descent of a roller coaster ride, terrifying at first but leveling off with time in flight. Most new experiences come with fear but if one projects to the excitement of a new adventure, most endeavors are tolerable, some enjoyable, even. Listen to this adventure story:

A twenty-year-old University of Michigan student found an opportunity to study abroad for college credit during the summer session of 1987. Not very wealthy, her experience in travel had excluded air travel until that time. For some, this may have been very difficult to maneuver, however, this student had always been like an Amelia Earhart in her doings and so her family begrudgingly allowed her to make her own way. She did not waver, even when she found that all of the direct international flights to Spain, the destination country, were completely booked. Her only option was to choose a flight going to Paris, France. From there, she would have to board a train and travel to her destination country. Never had she a course in French but was assured by friends that this was not a problem since everyone in the country is known to speak English.

This detour to France made for another prior-to-departure task. The student would have to obtain a travel visa in order to enter that country. Not only would she have to spend more money for the travel visa, she would have to leave Ann Arbor to travel to Detroit, where the nearest French Consulate was located. The young lady, not having transportation of her own, as did many of her school buddies, opted to take a passenger bus into the city of Detroit.

When the young lady boarded the passenger bus, it was quite full, however, a man who looked to be in his early thirties, allowed her to sit in the vacant seat beside him. With a bubbly personality and the excitement of the impending trip, she was friendly in her manner to everyone that she encountered. This particular encounter, however, was most intriguing.

The gentleman, seeming to be in need of a 'sounding board', leaned back fragilely, his frail and haggard personage in need of a small space of rest. The young lady allowed him to ease out his words, only voicing an occasional grunt or nod as he led the conversation.

"Do you have children?"

"No!" she laughed.

"I do" he returned. "Their mother and I do not live together. We are always fighting about something or the other…"

"Oh…"

"She's made a promise to me, though."

"Oh, yeah?"

"She's vowed never to have any other children by any other man. It's for the sake of the children, you know… She doesn't want them confused about different fathers. Having the same father will keep them together. She is not sure if she wants me back but she's adamant about that promise.

"She says that maybe later on, she would like to have more children and she would like to have me around — 'just in case…'!"

They both grimaced at that remark.

'What a profound philosophy!' thought the young lady. This was somehow an honorable rite. Maybe this is the way it should be. The prospect of not having battles among siblings about whose father is the worst or best deserved some consideration. The young lady suddenly found an admiration for this person that she had not yet even met, because of the profound maternal philosophy that seemed indeed unselfish.

Silence fell between the two for the remainder of the trip to Detroit. The young lady, however, gave much thought to what had been said, inwardly deciding that this was the way it ought to be.

On the ride to my apartment today, I witnessed the idea of cohesiveness that the gentleman spoke of in a family of geese. There must have been eighteen of these beings trying to find their way across the roadway. In the middle of the group was an injured member. Its foot was detached and the second half of the group awaited its arrival to the other side before making their own strides across. How noble!

Continuing with the young lady's preparation visit to Detroit, when she arrived at the bus depot in the downtown area, it was not much of a walk to the very tall Renaissance building. The structure of the building was very fashionable with deep plush carpeting and works of fine art decorating its many corridor walls. The young lady was in awe of its finery when she boarded the elevator, only to become even more impressed when she realized that the outer wall of the shuttle was made of very thick glass, making it possible to view the entire city on her ascent.

Her business of obtaining the French travel visa was handled with little difficulty. She presented her recently obtained United States passport along with the required application and fee. The booklet was inspected and stamped with the passage authorization. The lady student noted that they allowed ample time for her return flight from another French city, Nice. At that point, the young lady was not familiar with this city but after research, found that it was not many miles from the Italian border. She thought, "What a delight! I'll get to see three different countries on this visit!"

The day of the young lady student's departure was purely a frenzied rush. She had requested of her older sister a transport to the Detroit Metropolitan Airport terminal. They arrived very close to the scheduled departure time but were fortunate to find that the Pan American gate was almost immediate to where they entered the terminal. Quickly checking her bags and obtaining her boarding pass, she only had a few minutes to make her farewells.

She turned to her brother and sister with a wide grin, trying to hide her nervousness, thinking that this may be the very last time that they would ever see her alive.

She admitted, "I've never been on an airplane…"

The young lady student did not want to betray the feeling of excitement for the inward fear but thought that maybe these would be her last words and she needed to do something to try and calm herself.

"I thought you had flown, ____," commented her sister with a vote of reassuring confidence. "You'll be just fine!"

"Yeah, I'm just being silly…!" she thought to herself, brushing away the grip of fear before it could take root.

The best thing about her flight itinerary is that her first experience was very short in length, being that she had to take a commuter plane from the Detroit Metropolitan Airport to meet her connecting flight at the John Fitzgerald Kennedy Airport in New York City. The ascent into the air for the first time, however, was akin to the most formidable of roller coaster rides!

Today I discovered perhaps the main reason that depression has been allowed to have such a lasting grip on my life. I have been complaining about everything! I did not realize that this was something that actually makes a big difference in one's perspective. Complaints make me feel like everything has gone wrong and leave me feeling helpless. But I am not helpless - I can just stop complaining! Things are probably not going to change for the better or worse because of a complaint so I am just going to think of something else instead of the problem at hand.

I am very thankful that the move is finally over! It took a great deal of strength to make it happen. I thought that I needed to cry at some point but did not and now I am glad to have salvaged at least that one small piece of dignity. Self-pity can be both dangerous and volatile. Evidence of weakness can sink a ship on the brink of salvation. But I refused to let it happen this time around.

People with stern attitudes say that we need to just accept their decisions with serenity. Are they really happy when one refuses to beg or are they disappointed to have not felt the satisfaction of triumph in witnessing someone crumble before them? Is it for the benefit of doing what must be done that drives the harshness or is it the hunger for power and control over another person's destiny?

When the female student boarded the Pan-American 747 jet, leaving the John F. Kennedy airport in New York City, the excitement of the realized dream permeated through to the core of her being. There was not a familiar face anywhere! She looked down at her boarding pass and matched it to one of the center rows of chairs.

Although flying cabin class, the female student felt the most wealthy that she had ever felt in her life. She thought to herself. "I am going to Paris, the place where people dream of going to their entire lives! Wow! I'm REALLY going!"

When seated, the female student seized the opportunity to take in her surroundings, eyeing the massive volume of co-travelers who were murmuring while shuffling to their seats, preparing for the long trip ahead. Finally, hearing the purr of the large engines beneath her, the female student braced herself for the heave of the huge plane into the air. But to her surprise, the take-off was very smooth in comparison to her earlier plane ride. Of course most of the reason was due to the difference in the size of the flying vehicles but the number of passengers on board this large jet gave her a small comfort as well.

Not knowing anyone on board, the female student sat quietly for the first hour of the trip, occasionally rummaging through her bag, surveying her passport and the other items inside, mentally making a checklist of items that she might need to pick up once settled into her destination place. Finally, the male seated to her left spoke. She had noticed that he had taken a small nap since they had been in the air and now he looked sleepily around. It seemed that he, too, was traveling alone. As it turned out, he was a physician that had been visiting the United States for the purpose of attending a medical seminar on advanced medical technology. He was now headed for Paris to be with some of his family although he, himself, did not reside there. The physician's English was very limited as was the Spanish of the female student, but she graciously offered her Spanish as the language of communication, as this was the prime motive for her trip anyway.

Unlike the gentleman on the passenger bus, the physician offered nothing of his personal life into the conversation, mostly prodding the female student into answering questions about herself and her studies. She mostly talked about her life at the university, intentionally not letting on about her home-life, a little ashamed that she was not wealthy. She did not want to entice the tiresome teasing that she often endured in conversation around the college dormitory.

Soon it was announced that the flight movie would begin and again, a companionable silence fell between the female student and the physician.

When the jet finally landed at the Charles de Gaulle airport in Paris, France, it was mid-morning, marking more than twenty-four hours in travel for the female student. Collecting her bags from the baggage claim area, she noticed a sort of space ship feel in her surroundings that added to the now frightened feeling that she felt in the pit of her stomach. After going through Customs inspections and attempting to converse with travelers here and there, she found that these persons only spoke short sentences of English. Now, trying not to panic, she dragged her baggage with her as she hurried after person after person trying to find someone who could help her get into the city and onto the train to Spain.

"Hmmph! Where are all of the English speakers?! They must be sleeping!" thought the female student, discouraged.

"Where are you going?" asked a recently familiar voice from behind her.

The female student spun around to see the physician from the plane.

"Oh, it's YOU!" the female student sagged with relief. "Yo necesito un tren para Sevilla, Espana…" she started as the physician nodded to silence her into calm. He pushed her elbow forward in escort, propelling her toward the sub-trolley car's open doors. At this point, he was her only hope of survival because there was a huge ocean and thousands of miles between the female student and everything else that she had ever known.

As she sank into the sub-trolley seat, she fought to regain her optimism about this feat that she had taken on. Her physician host spoke French fluently as far as she could tell but looked very preoccupied about something and she felt that she had made herself a tremendous burden in her naïveté for having believed that she could arrive so ill-prepared to this place with the intention of success. The female student breathed in deeply the strong and strange aroma of the French outer city as the sub-train sped into the city's core.

Even though the physician admitted that he needed to leave directly to attend to other business, he insisted upon helping the female student check into a hotel so that she could tour the city. It would be such a shame to lose this opportunity so the young lady agreed hiding an inward caution of another unplanned expense.

The physician hailed a taxi and they traveled through the busy streets to a small but very clean 'hostel'. Once into the room, the physician announced that he needed to take his leave and left the female student alone for a much needed sleep.

CHAPTER SEVEN

Having left putting her things away until after her nap, the female student awoke with a start, at first confused by her surroundings in the dimness of the now evening hours. Leaping from the bed still fully clothed, she entered the adjoining bath. The 'bidet' was the first that she had ever seen and she wondered if it was there for washing feet since she had never heard of a toilet with faucet knobs. The room was equipped with the conventional shower stall and toilet so the female student ignored the presence of the bidet. She took a long warm shower to wash away the grime of travel and to revive her spirits. Soon, she emerged from the bathroom, feeling refreshed. She decided to wear a light-colored skirt, a violet silk top and sandals in celebration of a night in Paris.

The female student walked out onto the small balcony and leaning over the guard-rail looked at the surrounding buildings and the street below. It was strange to see only small motor cars, aged sidewalks and narrow, almost alley-like streets. She assumed that since European cities were well established before motor traffic, the widening of these roads was an impossibility. She was frightened for pedestrians who might lose their footing and fall into the path of one of the fast-moving motor cars. She decided to take a short walk to do some exploring on her own even though the physician had agreed to take her to the Eiffel Tower the next day. The female student grabbed her bag, locked the door, bounded down the stairs, passed the front desk with a smile and a nod and exited out onto the street.

The air had cooled but there remained a touch of humidity making the evening ideal for a short walk. The lady student mused at the different street ads and shops trying to decide on how to proceed, when not more than one-half hour into her walk; she spied a huge cathedral and decided to have a closer look. Hearing the chatter of other tourists and visitors, she identified the building as Notre Dame. Not far from the building, she spotted a vendor stand with postcards that confirmed her summation.

The female student removed her camera from her bag as she entered the dimly lit church, marveling at the fixtures of polished antique precious metal behind the gated stalls and altar. She spent the span of about an hour looking at the inner chapel and snapping photographs.

When the female student emerged from the church, she thought about making a detour for a bite to eat instead of going directly back to her lodgings. Instead, she made directly for the hostel discouraged by her lack of French-speaking ability and speculating that the English-speaking vendors would have higher prices.

To the pleasant surprise of the female student, there was a message at the front desk from the physician awaiting her upon her return. When she telephoned the number (thankful for English speaking desk staff), a teen male answered but recognized the name of the physician from the female student's request and soon the physician's voice came onto the line. He asked if she had eaten and with her negative reply, he stated that he would be over directly so that they could dine out.

"So this is where all of the American tourists hang out!" the female student thought the next day from the top of the Eiffel Tower.

The tower was much larger than she imagined, she noticed earlier standing next to one of the large foot-like pillars, looking up. The female student and the physician had walked to the bottom center of the structure and boarded the cage-like elevator, taking them to the very top. The lady student dashed from side to side of the quad-shaped level, taking in the view of the city from each. There were looks of surprise from the other tourists as she called to and chattered with the physician in the Spanish language.

"They are probably wondering why I am not speaking French!" the female student smiled to herself. After their descent, the female student and the physician crossed the acreage of well-manicured lawns to an entrance lot where dozens of artists were sketching and selling their artwork. The physician treated the female student to a caricature portrait of the lady prepared by one of the artists. The female student giggled at the very accurate capture of her person on the rolled paper in front of her,

"What amazing ability!" she mused.

The female student regretted that there was only time to view Sacre Coeur from the roadway as they rushed later on that day to meet her train that would carry her to Seville, Spain. However still, she was very glad that she had taken the recommended tour; she smiled as she clutched her miniature Eiffel Tower, the portrait and instant photographs souvenirs from the visit.

The female student was very grateful to the physician for lending his precious time to ensure her safety during her stay in Paris. She plugged his name into her permanent memory block and waved a vigorous goodbye as the train pulled away from the platform. The female student heaved a sigh of relief and leaned back for yet another long ride.

CHAPTER EIGHT

'Moroccans!' The female student had never even heard of the country of Morocco until now. The train car was filled with Moroccan students, all male, headed to their homeland for the summer break. One of the friendlier ones, sharing a booth with the female student, decided to be a spokesperson for the group. He was very thin and had long, dark curly locks of thick hair.

The friendly Moroccan disclosed that he and the other two male students, one wearing glasses, with an inquisitive look about him and the other, the tallest of the three, quiet and skeptical, were doing their studies in Paris. They all spoke an Arabic language and French. The friendly Moroccan spoke English as well. He offered his headphones to the female student so that she might sample the 'Moroccan-style rock-n-roll' played on the cassette tape inside of the pocket stereo. The female student listened to the stringed instruments evoke the shrilly twangs and the pounding beats of the percussion beneath the yodeling voice. She admitted that it would take a bit of getting used to and returned the headset to its owner. He really seemed to enjoy the lyrics that held no meaning for the female student.

"Ah-ah-ahi-si-oh-mai-mai-chiim-bii!" sang the friendly Moroccan. The female student smiled at his zest and excitement.

The temperature was scorching and the passengers took turns traveling up and down the corridor to cool off in the travel car that had no air conditioning. The female student had donned shorts and removed her shoes to try to get more comfortable.

The friendly Moroccan, prompted by his two companions, flashed a sly smile and asked the female student what was the most famous of American foods.

"We eat lots of different foods in America…" she began slowly, wondering what the humor was about.

"China and Japan have lot of rice and meat foods. In Italy, they make spaghetti. The French have much good cuisine. India has food with curry. Everyone, every country have special food, but America… HAMBURGER!!" announced the friendly Moroccan.

The female student was taken aback and tried not to appear insulted by this absurd summation of American culture and taste.

"We have more than that…" she faltered trying desperately to think of food entrees that did not belong to or originate in some other country. At present, she could not think of anything else that was exclusively American and gave an indignant grunt at the look of smug satisfaction on the faces of her male cohorts.

The female student refused to back down to this superiority ambush,

"We have other foods. You just would not know what they were if I were to name them!"

The friendly Moroccan smiled broadly at her lie and snatched the miniature Eiffel Tower statue that she had been holding.

"Give that back! I want my Torre Eiffel" the female student demanded, reaching for her treasure.

"I want my Torre Eiffel!" mocked the Moroccan rising to his feet and leaping up to stand on the seat cushion.

The female student refused to play this childish game knowing that it was a three-to-one competition. She stood standing with an angry stare while the long-haired Moroccan examined the statue leisurely, as if to train a wild stallion not to rebel. Finally, he handed the statue to her with feigned meekness.

The lady student took the object in hand briskly, resisting a most tempting urge to hit the smiling face in front of her.

The night air on the train was only slightly better than during the daylight hours. The four in the train booth car decided to send the two other student Moroccans to find other seats in the somewhat empty more expensive adjoining car, leaving the long haired and female student able to stretch out across the booth seats for a more comfortable slumber. It was not many hours into the night, however, when the two returned. The conductor had 'booted' them out of the quarters of the adjoining car, reminding them that their passage tickets did not afford them the right to be there. So fatigued was the female student, she just sat up right and fell back into sleep.

The female student awoke quite early the next morning. There was not much further travel to Seville. The scenery of the Spanish countryside was mostly filled with mountainous regions, so the long-haired Moroccan dragged out photographs

to show to the female student. While viewing the photographs, the female student noticed the diverse appearance of the many faces looking back at her. The Moroccan pointed out that there was not a separation among his people based upon skin hue or hair texture. The female student compared this way of thinking to the distinct separation of the American masses. The Moroccan unconditional acceptance of its entire human part was very admirable.

Soon the time arrived for the female student to disembark. Finally having arrived in Seville, she felt that she had really reached her destination much earlier for she had already learned so much from those that she had met on the journey.

CHAPTER NINE

Taxi cab fares! The clock on the dashboard seemed to roll at a phenomenal speed. The female student decided that she would have to find another, more economical means of transport after the very confusing and expensive ride from the train station. Finally, the very large doors of the Casa de Santa Maria swung open and behind them was a maid. She ushered the female student in to where the student was greeted by the program director,

"Eres muy bendita para llegar! Estamos agradecidos que estes aqui!" (You are very blessed to have arrived! We are grateful that you are here!)

The house was very lovely indeed! It was fashioned with a central atrium courtyard, equipped with a balcony on the second level overlooking the courtyard. The housekeeper led the female student to the above quarters where she was assigned a room with two other female students, one still sleeping in a narrow cot in the large bedroom. Quietly and carefully the female student unpacked and found the community bathroom to shower.

After having showered and changed clothing, the female student was no longer sleepy. She crept down to the lower level of the house and found the sitting room. Its only occupant at the time was an independent study student who invited the newly arrived to just relax and unwind since the morning classes were already in session.

The independent study student spoke the Spanish language incredibly well although not being of Latin descent. The female student was impressed by how well the other student could toggle between English and Spanish with ease and without a single tinge of accent carried over in the process.

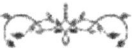

I have lost the vehicle that I was buying on an installment loan. This is for the best because it was just not affordable with the situation that I am in. A family member did offer me another vehicle which suits my immediate needs and I am grateful that things are starting to fall back into place.

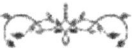

"The long haired Moroccan was right!" thought the female student when purchasing a 'whopper' at a Burger King restaurant in Madrid, Spain, paying double the price for which the sandwich sold in the United States.

The group had moved from the Seville location to spend a week in a hotel in the capital. Many of the students in the group had been able to visit the famous sites but our female traveler had been left behind most often because she had nearly depleted her travel budget. The remarkable fact was that Chinese food was more economical in Spain than in America and she had been able to, for the first time; eat in a Chinese restaurant for the equivalent of five American dollars!

UNSPOKEN LINGUISTICS

The program conductors, however, had allowed the entire group to sample the most famous of Spanish cuisine, *paella* and *gazpacho,* treating them to a group lunch in an elegant family restaurant during the stay in Seville. The gazpacho, a soup served cold, laced with onion and tomato was a surprise for our female traveler's taste buds! It was not as pleasant as the paella, a savory dish of yellow rice and seafood, seasoned with olive oil. Our female traveler, too, now longed for the American soft 'wonder' bread instead of the hard crusted loaves presented in this Spanish country.

The European coffee was indeed strong and our female traveler had to insist upon 'café con leche' instead of the coffee black for which she was accustomed in the United States.

Alcohol beverage intake did not exclude the youth. One bartender explained that if one was tall enough to order, they could buy the beverage of their choice. Spanish custom was to allow wine to be served during the family meals to everyone seated at the table.

Even with the loose ties of food and beverage intake, the Spanish youth seemed to be very well-mannered and without mischievous intent. One afternoon, our student traveler and a few others from the group decided to make a trip to the public pool. Not knowing how to swim, our student traveler remained at the shallow end of the pool where there were many small children who looked on with interest at this older occupant in the juvenile territory. A small lad, of about seven years of age, still wearing his glasses in spite of it being swim time, seemed to take a liking to our female traveler and followed her about until she finally inquired,

"Cual es tu nombre?"

"Juan Carlos!"

Our female traveler smiled in response. He must be kidding! Juan Carlos was the name of the Spanish king! Another female group member who had decided to move to the shallow end of the pool, seeing the doubtful expression on our female traveler's face, explained that it was common place to name children for the famous "Rey de Espana".

Well, this small 'king' had taken it upon himself to force our female traveler to swim as all adults should – without a floatation device. He made a chore of quickly snatching away the floating air tubes as they became available so that they were always out of the reach of our female traveler. This was frustrating, although a little comical to our female traveler. Finally, she managed to actually grasp one of the floating tubes that had been abandoned while the young 'rey' was not looking. At last, she could leave the shallow end!

"Damelo!" ordered the familiar voice of the rambunctious youth who suddenly appeared out of nowhere.

Our female traveler decided to surrender and exit the pool altogether, grateful that she now had a firm grasp on the Spanish language command form verb conjugation with the direct and indirect object order.

CHAPTER TEN

Autumn has arrived and the days now come with a brisk wind. The park playground is now vacant more often because the children are busy in preparation for school classes to resume. The rain has kept them away as well, making the days dreary enough for them to find things to do inside of their homes.

Perhaps the only warm clothing that these students possess is the newly purchased outfits that are reserved for the new school year. For school children, this is one of the biggest and exciting events of the year. Making a good first impression on the rest of the school body is not only important to the youngsters, it reflects upon the parents. This will often control how much influence their concerns will have upon the implementation of the child's educational strategy. A well-dressed child most certainly will acquire the backing of the school officials more so than a raggedly dressed and unbathed child. Dress is a large part of the social hierarchy mentioned earlier. In fact, some of the inner-city public schools have decided to mandate uniform dress codes in order to combat the rise of unrest that has been known to have been caused by competitive apparel.

Some parents have spent small fortunes replenishing clothing that has been stolen or rejected by other students. Rumors and mockery of poor personal hygiene and dress frequent the conversation of the middle and high school cafeteria area. Tables are even segregated based upon this same premise. An impoverished parent must possess great wisdom in order to render a child who is unscathed from 'dress' prejudice.

I have witnessed this wisdom in action on occasion. One farmer's daughter was only purchased a single pair of blue jeans and a variety of inexpensive tops to last throughout the school year. Each night she would hand wash the blue jeans and allow for them to dry during the night. Sometimes, she had to put them on, damp as they were, and still manage to make it on time to meet the school bus pick up. This female student was very quiet and remarkably amiable. Even those closest to her did not notice the lack of clothing. She was always bathed and had clean teeth. There were never rumors or mockery spread about her and her efforts were rewarded in some kind. Even more remarkable was that this young lass who was experiencing such tragedy of poverty, graduated from high school, not with honors, but without pregnancy. She was a heterosexual being.

Clothing donations in the thrift stores are often of the latest fashions. Many 'one-price' stores have emerged, helping low wage earning parents better afford school supplies to fit their limited budgets. However, the downside is that these vendors often get their merchandise from foreign suppliers which further deplete the nation of an already dwindling number of jobs. Like the high school student, perhaps the answer to achievement is in having limited resources. It is true for almost all that we tend to be somewhat careless when our supplies are plentiful. However, those who must survive with just a little, tend to make wiser choices about what goes out with the garbage. Of course, being one of the world's 'fortress' nations, we cannot afford to abruptly sever our ties with other nations.

I see the nations of the world as siblings of the same global family, yet as in any family, some siblings are more independent than others. Underdeveloped nations rely upon developed nations not only as monetary sources but as role models – of how they may become developed nations as well. We need to focus more so upon the idea of the latter. Being a developed nation does not mean that the United States Treasury can afford to pay for the upkeep of all of the third-world nations… Not when we have a population of our own to support. If citizens of third world nations have to work for a meager wage then they have something… Many Americans do not have employment at all.

Our capitalistic nation demands that American citizens compete for employment opportunities. Underdeveloped nations have to understand that the developed nations are able to bestow their rights to federal grants and loans because of monies gathered from taxpayers who must compete to earn their wages. These taxpayers must compete to get the job for which they must compete to be educationally qualified and they must compete to maintain employment.

It is easy to ignore poverty, especially when it exist thousands of miles away but the answer is not in persecuting those who come to us for help. We simply must find ways of 'teaching the poor man to fish' instead of buying him a meal.

CHAPTER ELEVEN

Salamanca is one of the many medium-sized but well-known cities located in the northern region of Spain. During the summer months, its temperatures are moderately cool in the evening hours, making a visit to the central 'Plaza' a welcomed social ritual after a day of classes. Although the University of Michigan students had now each been assigned to separate lodgings in different Spanish households, our female student traveler joined at least one of the others each night in the Plaza for late refreshments and or ales, to discuss plans for evening dances, messages from the States and for other miscellaneous light chatter. The Plaza, a very large arena was a large square in shape, having an arched entrance in each of the four corners of the structure. The court had no roof apart from the vendor stalls aligning its perimeter but was equipped with tile plates over the entire floor. Many sets of covered tables and chairs were posted in front of the food stands.

There is much to be observed of the lifestyle rendered by the socio-economic status of the Spanish household. Soon after settling into one of the guest bedrooms of the high rise apartment home of an elderly female whose only family appeared to be an absent son, our female student traveler decided that the clean but sparsely furnished domicile was evidence of very limited financial means. She looked on with pity and winced at the varicose veins rising up from the forefoot around the ankles of the elderly woman's high heel clad feet. Most of the adult women of Spanish society wore pumps in public places at all times and many that had aged and now walked with a slower pace, maintained this etiquette.

Personal automobile transportation was difficult to obtain as well for members of the Spanish population. Most families were limited to the ownership of one motor car. Many household members walked to their in-town destinations and traveled by passenger bus or train when the destination was located out of town. Telephone privileges were tapered to short conversations and were mostly in the business context. Residential phone service was a guarded rite because of the less than affordable rates. The urban residents often used the phone company building, the 'telefonica', to make phone calls both international and domestic. This was a large showroom somewhat like a bank lined with phone stalls as in airports or in hospitals but much more in abundance. Although these telephones could be used, telephone privileges were seldom used for social contact. This was one of the reasons why the gatherings at the Plaza were such an important part of Spanish residential daily regimen. Now living with a Spanish resident, the female student traveler noticed that food ingredients were exchanged and substitutes were included that were more affordable to the Spanish family budget. The elderly female host guardian was kind in asking the female student what food she had most enjoyed since arriving to 'Espana'.

"A mi, me gusta Paella!" (I like Paella!)

"Entonces, yo te prepare lo que prefieres para la cena!" (Then I will make it for dinner tonight)

"De veras?!" (Really?!)

"Si! De veras! Ahorita, yo lo prepare!" (Yes! Really! I'll make it right away!)

When the meal was served and the two were seated, the female student traveler eyed the food in front of her... The seafood was replaced with boiled eggs! Careful not to show ingratitude, the female student quickly scooped up a forkful of rice. It was tolerable, the flavor of the other distinguishing ingredients still carrying through from the original seafood recipe. The female student decided that she would make a special effort to enjoy the entrée prepared this way since her hostess had made it especially for her benefit. She, however, declined a second serving.

Days after, another female guest traveler joined the two in the apartment. She was from non-Flemish Belgium and was traveling alone. She spoke French and English but arrived in Salamanca with the intention of learning Spanish. The University of Michigan female student traveler tasked herself with translating communication between their hostess and the new arrival. The Belgian student offered verbal lessons of her native French to the University of Michigan student in return.

"JE-NE-PAR-LE-PA-FRANCE!" slowly coached the Belgian student.

"JE-NE-PAR-LE-PA-FRANCE!" repeated the Michigan female.

"What does that mean?" she inquired after a few practices with the phrase.

"It means 'I don't speak French!'" the Belgian student announced smiling at her clever christening method.

"Phew!!" the Michigan student let out a relieved breath. "That's a great place to start!"

They both giggled.

The Belgian student's visit to Salamanca was arranged and sponsored by her family. She would have to pay their hostess directly a nominal amount for her space and create her own study agenda. The Michigan student's boarding fees were paid by the university program coordinators so that previously she had expected to independently find another inexpensive hostel to stay after the program ended which left her with one week before her return flight to the United States was scheduled to leave. Now aware of the fee that the Belgian student paid was a practical amount, the Michigan student decided to make arrangements to remain in her current lodgings after her classes were concluded.

"JE-SCHWI-AMERICAN!" continued the Belgian student. "That means 'I am American!'"

"JE-SCHWI-AMERICAN!" repeated the Michigan student. "What do I say when I want them to stop because I don't understand?"

"JE-NE-COMPRE-PA!" replied the Belgian student. "That means 'I do not understand what you say!'"

"JE-NE-COMPRE-PA!" muttered the Michigan student quietly. Now she grabbed a pencil and paper realizing that this information was much too important to chance being forgotten.

"Now you have enough to approach them!" said the Belgian student. "Here we go!: 'JE-NE-PAR-LE-PA-FRANCE-PA-SE-CUER-JE-SCHWI-AMERICAN. JE-PAR-ENGLE-OO-ESPANOL!"

"Translate please!!!!?"

"That means 'I don't speak French because I am American. I speak English or Spanish!"

The Michigan student quickly scrawled the phrases with English and Spanish phonetics because she did not have familiarity with written French and did not wish to over taxi the other student with the already generous effort.

"You show much promise for French. You have a good accent and pronounce the words with good ability..." remarked the Belgian student.

"That's because you are a great teacher!" returned the Michigan student.

"Maybe..." hesitated the Belgian student. "Do you miss your boyfriend? I miss mine so-o much! He's such a wonderful, beautiful man!" she said, changing the subject.

"I don't have a boyfriend" replied the Michigan student. "I'm just enjoying traveling and studying for now. Does your boyfriend treat you well?"

"Oh, he is so lovely! We have a very good time together!"

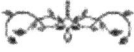

I am feeling that others around me have changed very much. Previously I felt that my presence was accepted with neutrality. Now I am often challenged to make difficult decisions. I'm finding it is expected for me to stay through to the completion of discussions —even for those that are insulting and threatening to me personally. It helps to be able to use these experiences as a reference when it is my turn to make decisions to buy from independent vendors. It makes perfect sense not to buy those girl-scout cookies when I've just been told that I make foolish purchases. Many times I have been restricted to the 'My way or the highway' ultimatum. When I have tried to reason with these persons about concluding a friendship tonight that may be needed tomorrow, the response has been: "Today is here and tomorrow is not!" So now I don't reassure myself with threats of revenge. I simply wait for the Sun. I now know that if I can fall asleep that the morning will come with new optimism. I've discovered that when faced with ultimatums that threaten my survival, however viable, I can refuse to allow anger to be loaded into my psyche. I now just tell myself that they are entitled or empowered to refuse me benefits, however I am allowed to not retaliate. Whether they want a violent response or not will best be left un-pondered. I have learned to wait until it is time for me to make a decision from my realm of authority to know what wiser decision the angry messenger was preparing me to make.

    "If you wish to introduce yourself in French, we say 'JE-MA-PELLE' with our Christian name behind it. For example: 'JE-MA-PELLE-MADAMOISELLE _____,'" allowed now the Belgian student.

    "JE-MA-PELLE-MADAMOISELLE_____" echoed the Michigan student as she continued writing. "Why am I not Madame?"

"When you marry, you will become Madame" answered the Belgian student. "Now you are ready; 'JE-TE-IDIOT! MENT-NOI-JE-SCHWI-INTELIGENT! PORQUOI? PA-SE-CUER-JE-PAR-FRANCE!' That means, 'I was unlearned but now I am wise! Why? I speak French!"

The Michigan student scrawled madly as her companion lectured and when there were pauses, she rehearsed these phrases.

"Yo voy para hablarla a la Senora. I am going to speak to the House lady" said the Michigan student now rising to leave the room. "Gracias para las lecciones-Thank you for today's lessons" She had grown accustomed to translating on occasion, introductory phrases even when speaking to her new French but English-speaking acquaintance.

When the Michigan student entered the other room, the Senora paused from cutting spices and wiped her hands on the front of the vested apron. Although there were no stairs to climb or wide rooms to cross in the apartment, the elderly woman was always winded with the slightest of movements.

'Perhaps she suffers from asthma,' mentally concluded the Michigan student again sympathizing at the tremendous amount of struggle that it took the Senora to maintain the extreme immaculacy of the living quarters.

Aloud she cautiously began "Me puedo hablar con Usted por favor?" (May I speak to you please?")

"Si! Claro! Cuales lo que deseas tu?" (Yes! Of course! What can I do for you?") smilingly welcomed her hostess in spite of the raspy voice with which she uttered.

"Mi vuelto viaje a los Estados Unidos falta una semana de salir despues que acaban mis clases…" (My return flight to the United States leaves one week after my classes conclude...), continued the Michigan student.

"De veras?" ("Really")

"Si. Yo quiero pedirla a Usted que me permitas quedar unos dias mas que ha pagado la Universidad y yo la pago a Usted directamente por lo que falta..." (Yes. I wish you to permit me to stay after the originally agreed upon time and I will pay what is owed additionally), rushed on the Michigan student before the courage could escape her.

The Michigan student had learned much about the mode of respect that was required in this place. It was extremely important that young maidens, especially, learn to keep their stares averted at all times and never look male encounters directly in the eyes. She had been cautioned by her University instructors that eye contact with the male species of this culture was viewed as an automatic sexual invite. The police authority would be pleased to act in a 'hands-off' or non-committal manner if a male accused of sexual harassment pleaded that the accuser had given him permission or 'the eye' and merely teased and baited his affections. The expected code of conduct was very much the foundation of one's success in this European country. The maturely wise women were selective in approaching even *female* travelers but if the foreign female showed herself harmless, responsible and respectful, these older women would make much effort to groom the female traveler to the courtesies and mannerisms expected of her in their society. The Michigan student did not wish to lose this protective device by appearing to be less than independent. So, it was with great care that she voiced her request as a possible offer instead of a plea for assistance.

Although there were males that showed interests around her, the Michigan student had no intention of prioritizing possibilities over the somewhat established arrangement of the space provided by the elderly woman.

"Usted quiere quedar aqui por unos dias mas? Cuanto? …para saber la cantidad yo… (You wish to remain a few days more? How many? I need to know for billing how many days specifically) urged the Senora without a commitment yet.

'Yes! She's actually considering accepting my offer!' thought the Michigan student with relief. Aloud, she moved on still hurriedly, "Yo quiero salir cinco dias despues que acaban mis clases pero insisto que yo pague para la semana la entera si me de Usted la oportunidad de quedarme. (I would like to remain for five days after my classes are concluded but I insist paying for the entire week if you will allow me the opportunity to stay). The student still struggled to keep a professional tone in her voice not wishing her hostess to feel obligated and not wishing to appear juvenile.

"Entonces. Te permito quedarte aqui los cinco dias mas. Pero Usted me pague ahora para mantener el espacio. La cantidad es catorce mil pesetas. De acuerdo?" (Well then… I will allow you to remain here for five additional days. But you must pay now to reserve your space. The required amount is one hundred forty dollars. Agreed?)

The Michigan student was very disconcerted but tried to recover her confidence to object, "Mi companera Belgica dice que paga ella solo doce mil pesetas!!?" (But my friend from Belgium states that she only pays $120 for one week!!?)

"NO-NO!" the elderly woman shook her head from side to side vehemently to firmly clarify, "La Universidad paga catorce mil pesetas para Usted y Usted paga lo que pagan *ellos*!" (The University of Michigan pays one hundred forty dollars per week on your behalf and you must pay what *they* pay on your behalf!)

The Michigan student was somewhat dispirited but meekly consented to the arrangement with the proposed fee.

CHAPTER TWELVE

Although the Michigan student was disappointed about the twenty dollar difference in rate, she knew that the amount was indeed competitive with other possibilities that she would find on her own. She was merely saddened that she had incorrectly assumed that she would be offered the same rate that the Belgian student paid. She also felt ashamed that she had revealed that she had been told it by the other girl and perhaps had betrayed a trust by accident. Her intention had not been to create an animosity but the price quote had taken her by surprise and there came with the protest the information shared by the other young lady.

To the relief of everyone, the conflict did not last beyond the conversation on the exterior and so the Michigan student continued in her congenial way among the other two women. However, another financial conflict arose soon after. The Michigan student used the laundry facilities regularly in the elderly woman's apartment as part of the lodging agreement. One afternoon, the Senora requested that the Michigan student come to speak with her in the kitchen, privately.

"Es importante que Usted mire un problema que traspaso' despues que Usted uso' el secadora. Parece que esta' rota la banda adentro dice el mecanico y lo que debe para arreglarlo es seis mil pesetas. Yo necesito que usted pague la cuenta por que la culpa es la suya." (It is necessary that you have a look at a problem that occurred when you used the dryer. It appears that the band inside of the machine has broken says the repairman and it will require sixty dollars to repair. You must pay for the damages because it was from your items that it broke) explained the Senora.

"Como-Como?!" (What?! How?!), responded the Michigan student, confused.

The elderly woman stopped in front of the machine and opened the door to indicate its back panel. She held up a small wire that had been laying on top.

"Esto…! De la sujetadora. Se paro' adentro!" (This…! From your brassiere was detached and broke the band!), concluded the Senora.

"Seis mil pesetas? Tengo que pagar *yo*? (Sixty dollars? Why must I pay?), stammered the Michigan student, shocked by the announcement.

"Porque resulto' de lavar la ropa de Usted! Por favor, Pagalo!" (You must pay because *your* clothing made the damage. Now, Please pay!), demanded the elderly woman.

"Why is she insisting that I pay?!" thought the Michigan student trying to think up a possible defense. This new bill would leave her with only enough to pay for her train ticket for her return flight to the United States! Of course, the Michigan student knew not to reveal that she was so low on funds because as earlier mentioned, this would leave her with a vulnerability that she could even less afford.

"Me permita Usted ver el pedazo del fierro para veriguar que es mio?" (May I have a closer look at the wire object so that I can identify it as mine or not?), the Michigan student tried again, extending her hand out for the wire.

"Pues, claro! Por su puesto es lo suyo!" (Of course! It's definitely from your clothing!!), said the Senora placing the small wire into the waiting palm of the Michigan student's hand. "Seis mil pesetas es lo que debe Usted el mecanico. Por favor, Pagalo!" (The bill is sixty dollars. Please Pay!)

The Michigan student examined the wire and conceded that it belonged to her. What she wasn't convinced of is that this small object had been solely responsible for the breakdown of the machine.

"No puede ser, posiblemente, la culpa de otra cosa? ...Es tan pequenita esta cosa..." (Perhaps something else broke the machine? ...This is so delicate and small...), observed and cautiously commented the Michigan student.

"No, no es otra cosa!" (It was that wire!), declared the Senora firmly shaking her head from side to side. She closely pursued the Michigan student in the circular back and forth pace around the table as the conversation had been taking place.

Again, feeling as if it would be of no affect to continue the discussion, the Michigan student again relented and agreed to pay the bill.

Classes were scheduled to be concluded in only two days and the University of Michigan students sat in the 'Plaza' that afternoon discussing plans for departure. One of the students, who had purchased a 'Eur-Rail' train travel passage authorization which offered almost unlimited two week travel to and around most of Europe, noticed that our female traveler was not eating or drinking. Our student had never complained or asked any of the others for money but it was noted that she did not purchase souvenirs or go off on weekend excursions as did her classmates.

"Are you in need of money?" inquired the student with the passage authorization.

"I am just now…" quietly admitted our female traveler. "But I'm fine. I will have to ask my mother to get money wired to me…" she hurriedly added so that the others wouldn't start into a scrutiny of her financial status.

"Isn't wiring money expensive? Oh-No! You should not require your mother to do that! Listen: I have to write a large personal check from my bank account in the United States and my American Express charge card will pay for me to cash it here. How about I write if for $100 more? Is that enough? Your mother will only have to get the money to my mother so that the funds will be available when my check is presented at my bank for payment!"

"Is it that easy to do?" responded our female student traveler surprised by the offer but not wanting to appear anxious to accept assistance.

"Yes, of course! It's not difficult. Just give me your mother's name and telephone number and let your mother know that they need to arrange payment from there" reassuringly answered the female with the Eur-Rail passage authorization.

"Are you sure it's no problem?" our female traveler insisted.

"No problem! Let's go to the 'Exchange' now!" invited the student with the Eur-Rail travel passage authorization rising from her chair.

Our female traveler, somewhat stiffly, arose too and fell into step with the other student. Minutes later, they arrived at the 'Exchange' and our female traveler quietly waited just inside the entrance while the student with the Eur-Rail travel passage authorization completed the necessary business transactions. Later when they had emerged from the building, our female traveler offered a small piece of paper with her mother's name and telephone number carefully written and the student with the Eur-rail travel passage authorization gave to her the $100 already replaced into Spanish currency.

"Let's call our mothers now!" instructed the student with the Eur-Rail travel passage authorization heading in the direction of the 'telefonica'.

When our female traveler had spoken to her mother, she replaced the receiver and went in search of the other student. She found the other young female still deep in conversation, a perplexed look on her face. The student with the Eur-Rail travel passage authorization concluded the conversation and turned to face our female student traveler.

"My mother is very upset that I wrote the check without speaking to her about it first. She says that I'm going to be in great trouble with the bank! I do hope that your mother gets the money to her today!"

"Shall I return you the money…?" helplessly offered our female traveler.

"No. The check has already been written. Are you sure that your mother can get the money there today?" pressed the other young lady.

"Yes. I'm sure that she'll get the money to your mother…I'm sorry for the trouble…" apologized our female traveler.

Again, she was in a conflict regarding money. These situations always seemed to remind her of the less than 'comfortable' socio-economic status that she had inherited at birth and its *many* boundaries.

When the other students had gone, our female traveler busied herself with plans for last minute sight-seeing opportunities. Most of the town had been roamed but now the Michigan student took daily strolls around its outer wings. She could relax a bit more with the money that she needed in hand but was still very careful and protective of it. She had put off sending post cards; one-because she hadn't dared be confident enough to guarantee her arrival with so many possibilities of failure and secondly-with postage considered, postcards were hardly more economical than souvenirs. Our traveler decided, however, to send a few cards with brief and happy messages but primarily occupied her time snapping photographs for memoirs.

She had confirmed with her mother that funds had reached the other student's mother for a timely deposit, but was instructed to just get back home with no more incidents or inconveniences. And she did that. Straight away she went about purchasing her train ticket.

Our female traveler had been so protective of her funds that she did not meet many males but she did achieve a brief friendship and acquire the admiration of a resident student. His mother was not from Spain but her sister, his aunt, resided there and his father was from Portugal, the neighboring country. The two students enjoyed walking and talking as they looked out over the picturesque scene of mountains that bordered the outskirts of the city. Our female traveler, having arrived at night with the group and asleep until the passenger bus came to a halt at the station in town had not noticed the abrupt transition from uninhabited terrain to the heavily populated suburbs. The outermost buildings were bordered with deserted fields. It was noted that farmland in this country was situated at a distance from the metropolitan areas, some even atop smaller mountainous regions where there were clear freshwater lakes for irrigation but low altitudes with enough warmth in the atmosphere for plant survival. One could see farmers that looked sometimes indigenous work the land with the assistance of oxen and other beasts as in the primitive way instead of with modern machinery.

"Nos casemos!" announced the young male student unexpectedly the afternoon before our female traveler was scheduled to leave for Nice, France.

"Estas bromeando??!! …Yo vivo en los Estados Unidos!" replied shyly the Michigan student regarding the invitation as absurd but indeed flattering. Never had she received a marriage proposal feigned or legitimate.

Her male companion's request was from the legitimate realm however not realized at this point. He was studying aviation and hoped to earn a pilot's license. He, now with sincerity, promised to marry our female traveler when his certification and training were finished. The Michigan student listened with newly acquired interest to her companion's dreams and expectations for their shared future. Apparently, he had previously given thought to career and family before they met and had only left finding a 'Mrs.' or 'Senora' to fill the vacancy in his planned outlines. She *had* recently considered a concentration in the field of Spanish and with it would likely require more visits for study. She knew that there were internship opportunities that were sometimes available as well. For this reason, she did not dismiss the possibility of a future marriage with the young male student. After all, he was not presenting her with an engagement ring or asking her to cancel her return travel arrangements at present, was he?! No! However, for her to savor the friendship and to have a writing correspondent gave her the ambition to gracefully accept the agreement to write from home.

The young male student accompanied our female traveler to the train station for a late evening departure, he carrying the heaviest of the young lady's baggage. He helped her to load her things into a storage bin but could not locate seating as the passages had been overbooked and many who had boarded were standing in the aisles.

"No te preocupes. Yo voy estar bien. Ahorita, bajate! Esta saliendo el tren!," (Don't worry. I'll be fine. Now go! The train is leaving!), said our female traveler as she pulled herself from their warm goodbye embrace.

"Yo te escribo!" called her companion as he obediently disembarked, stepping back down the small stairway onto the platform.

Away rolled the train into the night and even though the Michigan student had not yet exited the Spanish border, it was farewell to this country and its people for now.

CHAPTER THIRTEEN

Pable Italiano?"

"What? Como?" the Michigan student looked up and around, trying to pull away from her own thoughts. She had not found a seat even after the train had left the station in Salamanca and now sat cross-legged in front of one of the aisle windows. She was indeed sleepy but dared not allow herself to fall asleep here. Earlier during the night, she had in a moment of desperation, decided to sneak into a vacant seat for the first class passengers to fall asleep, as with the previous train ride from Paris but had been promptly awakened and asked to present her passage ticket. The ticket inspector shook his head and motioned for her to move out from the compartment. She was not scolded severely for her wrongful occupancy; however, she was now very sure of the rules of passage and knew that she would not try to sneak into one of these compartments again.

"Pable Italiano?" repeated the voice and this time our female traveler realized that it belonged to a young man seated on the floor of the aisle approximately three feet from where she sat. There were four or five others resembling the speaker around him and the Michigan student frowned as she moved a quick glance over their faces before responding warily. "No hablo Italiano!" she ventured understanding the question because of the language similarity of Italian to that of Spanish but having only the ability to respond in Spanish.

The male speaker, not discouraged by the language barrier continued to speak to the Michigan student.

"Conoce (co-no-she) Italia?"

"No. Yo no conozco Italia" the Michigan student shook her head from side to side. "No mas que en los libros y la television."

This arrangement seemed to be suitable for our female traveler to converse lightly with the Italian male. They all vied for an opportunity to talk to her as if to know her was to know America.

The dim lights of dawn now appeared on the lower panel of the dark wall of sky in the east announcing the early morning's arrival. The train had now entered 'Pais Vasco', a region that was formally part of geographic Spain but very different in its culture and language. The dialects spoken in Castilla, northern Spain and Andalucia, southern Spain were recognizable to the typical Spanish speaker, however, the Vasquen language seemed to have no linguistic connection to that Spanish.

As the train slowed, a young male prepared to leave by gathering his baggage and moving toward the exit doors nearest the female traveler. The Italian males spoke to the young male preparing to exit but he did not understand them. Our female traveler attempted to communicate in English as well as Spanish but still he refused to make any effort to speak to any of them. After his departure, one of the Italian males informed our female that Vasquens can understand other languages but are advised to not let on to what they know. For that reason, the Michigan student did not feel slighted for long, allowing that it was a cultural implication and not a personal insult.

The train was expected to take the Italian males as far as Milan just inside the Italian border; therefore they were to continue on their way as later that morning the train pulled into the station in Nice, France. Now our female traveler bid farewell to the Italians and took her turn down the small stairs and onto the platform.

'What a beautiful place! It is so-o clean!' thought the Michigan student as she now sat beside one of the windows of the large jet buckled up and ready for take-off. And it was the best way to view the last glance of Europe for the first time. Nice was an exclusive and immaculate, quiet city situated on the coast and it was speculated to be home to some of the country's most wealthy. Our female traveler made content with just a sip of its fresh morning air as the train station was a short distance to the airport.

Now she clutched the handles of the armrest and looked out of the window as the jet circled around the runway positioning itself for its turn in the line of flying vehicles.

"Boooom-boooom-booom-booom---booo!" pounded the fast-moving wheels as the engines beneath hummed in time to catapult the machine, up-up-up-zooom into the air!

"Thanks for everything!" thought the Michigan student as she finally nodded, fatigue finally overtaking her.

It had been a great journey of learning and she had enjoyed the privilege but now focused on the return to her native land.

"Thanks for everything!" she repeated as she fell into slumber.

'What a mess!' inwardly panicked the Michigan student. The United States Customs was not moving very quickly on their inspections and the Michigan student fidgeted and paced in circles as she waited in line, thinking only of the short amount of time before her connecting flight was scheduled to leave, most likely without her. She had been told that there was no way to speed things up to accommodate her specific travel plans. She did not complain any further and just continued to wait her turn. Finally, she was given the clearance and tried to sprint to the gate where her flight was boarded and ready to leave.

Kirplunck!! she stumbled and fell onto the hard waxed floor. She was not hurt. Just wounded pride. "What else?!!" she asked herself as she groaned and rose embarrassed from the ground. She had missed the connecting flight.

Our female traveler went to the gate and made the necessary arrangements to catch the next flight going to the O'hara airport in Chicago, Illinois. She would need to call her mother to let her know that she was back in the States, however, she would be leaving for Southern California for another week's vacation before classes resumed for the fall semester. She had booked passage for a very low price prior to leaving for Europe so that she would not have to cancel the trip due to the shortage of funds that she had experienced there.

"I'm back in the U.S. but I'm delayed in New York" she announced when her mother's voice came onto the line.

"Oh! I was so-o worried. There was a plane crash in Detroit- a Northwest flight… there were a lot of casualties! I thought maybe it was somehow your flight."

"Ooh! How terrible! …No, I'm fine!" the Michigan student replied as her mother continued with the details. It was reportedly a piloting error that happened within the landing and take-off area of the airport and had resulted in the deaths of many passengers and bystanders that were commuting on the interstate route in front of the airport when the plane fell to the ground below. The Michigan student was very sorry for the tragedy but had established an acceptance of fate and travel. Having now some flight experience of her own, she had no qualms about continuing with her flight itineraries as scheduled.

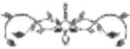

I am without employment again. I have a place to sleep for the present but tensions are rising and so I find myself sometimes sleeping in my automobile. One night, I awoke to see white all around me and the frost was inside of the car. My heater isn't functioning so my only protection from the cold is a warm blanket. It is fortunate that the worst of the winter weather has passed and nights are more tolerable. I've had to be more creative in choosing my activities because my income is very small but there has been more time to write. However difficult, I do have to plan an activity that keeps me away from the house until nightfall. It is best to have the practice and the discipline provided by having to plan winter excursions so that the summer's increased availability of free or inexpensive activities may compete with visiting and spending time with loved ones during the warm months even if they are not able to afford air-conditioning. Possibly, loved ones want me to prove my loyalty and devotion- they want to know that I will allow them to choose someone else for the opportunity that I wanted but accept the privilege of their company when it comes at a higher price.

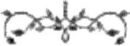

"Do they all look for *fame*...?" pondered the Michigan student as she walked through a mall close to the home of one of her sisters who lived in Santa Monica, California. She covertly eyed a voluptuous young woman posed like a statue on a stone brick island that included a fountain in its center. The other young woman didn't appear to be there with the purpose of shopping but seemed to be waiting for a talent scout instead. With good reason, the Michigan student decided that she would not seek fame for her own beauty considering that those who lived close to success headquarters seemed to be in an infinite queue in front of all others. For the moment, the greater of her concerns was protecting the single twenty-dollar traveler's check that remained of her travel funds.

Trying not to burden her sister and brother-in-law with the extra chore of providing an entertainment agenda for her visit, she volunteered caretaking responsibilities for her niece and nephew. For the first few days, she and the youngsters spent most of the afternoon at the nearby playground.

"JE-NE-PAR-LE-PA-FRANCE" the Michigan student prompted her nephew. Although both her sister and brother-in-law earned considerable wages, it was slightly evident that the tuition expense for the private French academy was a strained financial commitment for the family budget. The Michigan student was delighted to know of their scholastic curriculum. Now she tried her newly acquired phrase to know if she could pronounce it with enough skill to be recognizable to the ears of the child.

"You don't speak *any* French...??" responded her nephew, more interested in his play as he squinted his eyes at his aunt standing with her back to the sun.

The Michigan student smiled, feeling her face grow warm with embarrassment that she had been so confident with her new French vocabulary, but her nephew, although quite young was so quickly and easily able to respond to her statement. The youngster raced away at top speed, his sister running close behind, in the direction of the seesaw.

The Michigan student noticed that her nephew was quick to interpret the actions of the adults around him and had been taught to be responsible in play.

"People are tired and they are sleeping!" her nephew scolded his younger sister mimicking the words of his mother for when they were too loud in the mornings when she arrived from work and was in need of sleep.

From the nursery window, the Michigan student viewed the city of Los Angeles below in the distance with its foggy gray haze hovering above its perfectly planned and geometrically formed streets. It looked very much like a blueprint in its neatness and spacing of the buildings and roadways. At night, its lights looked like a collection of airport runways placed side by side. It was a contrast to the European roadway structure and one could easily identify the west coast format of landscape and architecture. The wide streets and large distance between the homes of the suburbs was a luxury in comparison to the close proximity of the suburban homes of the east coast.

Even with its wide streets, the skillful driver is needed to handle its inner-city traffic as well as its high mountain winding roads that sometimes have no guardrails. The adobe building material exterior is specific to the west coast in lieu of the Midwest wood slates, brick and vinyl siding used for building exterior. Also room size on the average is larger in the homes of the west coast than we find in the east coast residential home – Possibly a consideration of the higher cost of living when we contrast the space to some very small efficiency apartments on the east coast. Finally, it was remarkable to see that the natural lawns of this west coast region were as green as football turf. Lastly, although there were palm trees, they didn't seem to be abundant as in the state of Florida.

I had a very strange purchase experience yesterday. I thought that the laptop computer that I had been considering would be very easily purchased and the paperwork would give me adequate protection and assurance even if it were a cash purchase. I opted to go to a department store located in a city further away than the neighboring town because I had already visited the more local franchise earlier in the day and did not feel at ease to return that same day.

When I arrived at the electronics section of the store, I did not find the machine with the competitively low price that I had observed at the local department store. I felt the need to make the purchase at that store, so I decided to buy the next lowest-priced computer. I went in search of an attendant and asked if he could remove the item from the case. He looked below and mentioned that the one that I selected was not in stock but they had many of the next higher-priced unit with a different brand name. I explained that the first item requested was my limit for purchase dollars.

Disappointed, I decided to go to another store but the attendant asked if I would allow him to phone one of the other stores to find out if they had them in stock. After some phone calls, he came back with the news that the other stores in the chain in that city didn't have the one I wanted either, however, another store location out of town did have some and would be willing to set one aside for me if I were planning to buy today.

It was out of my way, but I did need to make the purchase and gave my name to this attendant to give to the attendant of the other store. **I thought that my concept of the value of money must be really off balance because I considered that my purchase intent was a large commitment and that I would not have much competition in deciding to spend so much money on one item.**

I left the store and rode onto the expressway in the northern direction somewhat assured of the other store's location but not entirely confident because of only having visited there one or two times prior to today. I did find the store with just a small amount of difficulty; however, the store attendant did not appear to have any knowledge of the arrangement to put aside a machine for me. He did agree to go back to the stockroom where he mentioned there were many of the model type that I wanted in storage to get one for me.

He was away enough time for me to test the machine type that I had selected on the display counter. My experience with laptop computers has been limited but was sufficient enough to allow me to navigate through the menu and applications to know that the word processing program could be adapted to accommodate my needs.

I had discovered that the installation of the necessary office application was a possibility from my brief survey and test run when the attendant reappeared with an armful of boxes, offering me one from the top. As he completed the sale, he asked if I would like to purchase a warranty and not having enough money in my budget, I declined the offer. I paid cash for the item and was given a small receipt to accompany my purchase.

I requested that the attendant allow me to open the box since the sale was complete to witness that nothing else would have to be purchased like additional cords before I left the store. I did inventory of the items inside of the box and looked through the paperwork, deciding that I had everything that I needed to get started, however still I felt uneasy about only having the tiny piece of paper without my name on it as proof of my purchase.

I turned around and inquired about the warranty. There was no way that I intended to leave the store without some type of paper-trail in accompaniment of that amount of money spent. I was told that I could still purchase the warranty but must go to the front of the store to the customer service desk to have the change made.

I decided to use a travelers' check to pay for the warranty for some type of evidence that it was I that had made the purchase because even with the warranty there was no identification required or requested to complete the sale.

I was assuring myself that I would be alright with the travelers' check as evidence of my connection to the purchase when just inside the exit door an alarm sounded and I was stopped by an elderly greeter and asked to present my receipt. She inspected my purchase and logged the incident on the paper on the clipboard she was holding.

How unusual! It seems that there are security devices in place but not the types that are easily identified and that lets us know that special attention has been paid to ensure that those who may be tempted to commit inappropriate acts against property owners are less likely to understand the security system to evade detection and surveillance.

The effort to produce security methods that are difficult to predict in a step by step manner by conspirators is important for the survival of businesses. Conspirators often identify commonly used practices to know the most vulnerable segments of time that exist in our daily regimens or processes so that they may thwart our attempts to maintain awareness of what is going on around us. The thought of making such a large purchase commitment compromised my attention to the amount of security that is undetected for these types of purchases. **I thought that I was the only one who would purchase this type of item on such a small budget.**

I did not feel the readiness to leave the store until I was sure that my investment was protected from potential loss. When I got into the car, I thought about going to the mall to get started but finally parked outside of a competitor's store to see if there was some way to separate the contents so that I would be more at ease to leave the box in the car while I went into the store.

To my pleasant surprise, I was able to register the computer right there in the car because the battery pack was already charged in the wrapped package. When I had finished with the registration, I placed the machine into a book bag and flung it over my shoulder to take into the store with the assurance that I would have media to present if questioned by the store personnel but not having to think about the new purchase being left behind in the car.

CHAPTER FOURTEEN

"How was Spain?!" inquired a young man whom the University of Michigan student had known since early childhood as he leaned in for a warm hug. He played piano for the church during praise and worship services and was a popular favorite especially among the young females. Now he teased our traveler with staccato spacing between his words to emphasize them.

"I have pictures!" grinned the University of Michigan student in response. She didn't get to see these people much since she had gone away to college and her home was a two-hour commute from school. It was New Year's Eve and her family had been invited to the home of a couple that lived in Kalamazoo, a mid-sized city less than thirty miles from her home. They were all warmly greeted and welcomed into the large den where everyone was partaking in conversation, food, drinks and refreshments. The house was very beautiful. It was a newly built and purchased two-story ranch house with a brick trim base that looked like a warm cottage smiling out from its blankets of white snow around its surfaces. It was a very quiet and popular subdivision and the University of Michigan student could only dream to work toward settling into one of its like types when she was ready to be wed.

"Where's the book?!" coaxed one of the University of Michigan student's sisters that was also in college but attending Western Michigan University also located in Kalamazoo. It was such a large gathering that the two had opted to sit on the floor near the huge fireplace where they now were busy answering questions about school and study plans. Their host scampered and crouched here and there all around snapping photographs during the festivities while his wife rushed around making sure that everyone was having a good time.

The University of Michigan student had placed the developed photographs from her trip abroad into a large binder-type photo album with a sturdy blue jean cover for protection. The book was passed from person to person while three or four others looked on, occasionally asking the University of Michigan student to explain the location or identify some of the selections. They were all full of questions about the people, places and the food entrees, clearly happy to know that one of their own had been allowed to accept such an opportunity.

"Who's this?" lightly scrutinized the young man piano player pointing at a young man with long hair pictured in one of the photos with the University of Michigan student standing laughing beside.

"Oh... That's just a friend that I met when we were out singing in the night club~!"

"Night club?~!"

"Yes! There are night clubs in Seville and this particular one had a disc jockey that sings really well. Anyway, I was invited to sing sometimes and it was a lot of fun!"

"We had better keep an eye on you!" chided the young man piano player. Although the University of Michigan student was now an adult, it remained a rite of her close family and friends to keep a 'watchful' eye out for her best interest.

The children of the host couple were very pleased to have so many people in their new home and went about helping their parents with the serving responsibilities, even the eldest son who was somewhat handicapped with mild mental retardation. It appeared that the couple had worked many years to have possession of this lovely abode and the University of Michigan student was very pleased for their happiness.

"Your mother says that you had to go to Paris, France first?! What happened?" inquired the mother of the piano player.

"Oh, it was fine! I panicked a little when I got there because I couldn't find a translator but thankfully someone did come along to help. So, I'm back in one piece!"

"Well, we are all glad for that! I do hope that you'll stay put for a while now~!"

"Uhm-m, actually I am thinking about another trip next summer…" confessed the University of Michigan student.

"O-oh!!" they all murmured in surprise, looking around at each other, exchanging glances.

The University of Michigan student knew that they were all just concerned about her well-being. She meekly acknowledged that the plan was only in consideration at present and accepted their caution for thought. But it did happen. At the end of April 1988, the University of Michigan student was again enrolled for the summer program in Spain.

ASSUMPTIONS.

I thought their home was empty, so I threw a few stones through the windows.
I thought their home was empty because there were no lights on, only shadows.
I thought that their furnishings were no match for down to earth people like me.
I thought that their clothing was not a dutiful investment as clothing needs to be.
I thought that their conversation was not humble enough for my children's ears to hear.
I thought that the neighborhood might be more peaceful if they were not so near.
I thought their home was empty, when the rage of fire started inside.
I was shocked as much as anyone else when someone told me they all died.

To have an understanding of utter fatigue, one could, perhaps, endeavor to work a 40 hour per week night job, a part-time job for college work study and attend college classes full time. Our female traveler fastened her two-way monitor to the belt of her security guard uniform, smoothing down the starched cotton top while shuffling her legs to straighten the meticulously ironed creases of her dark slacks.

"Another spooky night...!" muttered our female traveler, quickly surveying her black hard-toe shoes for scuffs and then flinging the key-clock over her neck onto her shoulders. She had to muster up courage every night to turn all of her keys, obscurely placed throughout her route before morning the next day. She especially paused nervously and looked closely all around when she made the key at the top of the Kresge Research Building on the medical campus of the University of Michigan. Its utility room was situated on the roof, carrying ominous sounds from the shadows behind the large boilers to our Michigan student's ears as she made her way to the back of the room to turn the key. She was insistent that she not have financial complications on this second trip to Europe. Working at the homeless shelter association for her work study grant helped her to pay for her pre-trip fees and daily living expenses while the night security job paycheck was used to purchase travelers' checks for her use while studying abroad.

Our Michigan student had awakened with a quick rush of blood to the temples of her head that stretched down to redden her entire face, making her head ache so intensely that it hurt to open her eyes. It had been one of the long days in which she had only time on her schedule to sleep for one and one half hours and often in trying to jolt awake too quickly, came this painful effect. It was worth the benefit to do this for her financial security on the second trip to Spain, after all it was only three days per week that she had to do all three responsibilities of her agenda.

It was good for the esteem of the Michigan student to travel because it was something different from the norm but for many, a competitive strategy for success. Her family had now become more relaxed with her intention for independence and this time she purchased one of the Eur-Rail travel authorization passages so that she could travel to see some of the other European countries after classes were concluded there. On this itinerary, was a direct flight to Madrid, Spain, however, the return flight was arranged to leave from Paris, France to return to the United States.

The Michigan student's celebrated success as a traveling student was complacent enough for her arrival to the Detroit Metropolitan Airport to be late and her flight again was already on the runway by the time she reached the gate. She was the one to blame even though the same of her sisters had driven her to the airport for this second trip but was thankfully glad that another flight could be arranged to meet with the overseas jet in New York city, New York. The only adjustment that would have to be made is for her to arrange for a taxi cab ride from the La Guardia Airport to the John Fitzgerald Kennedy airport because the substitute flight was to land at the La Guardia airport instead of the JFK where the overseas jet was scheduled to depart.

As far as the personal items loaded into her luggage bags, our Michigan traveler was more equipped to make this study trip, however, seeing the wreaths along the expressway marking the deaths of the previous year's travelers' from the August 1987 flight was a reminder that we don't have guarantees for survival in air travel.

One of the comforts that she had to be thankful for was that she did not have to arrange to store her personal belongings in her mother's home while she was away for the summer. The apartment had been subleased to other students and our traveler had continued with her rental agreement on the couch for the spring semester of classes and the new occupants had agreed to allow her to store her belongings there while she was away so that she had one less thing to do on her already impossible schedule. She had given charge to one of the previous roommates to find the two an apartment rental for the fall 1988 term in her absence. She had written to the male admirer in Salamanca to let him know that she had a confirmed schedule for arrival and he agreed to see her again this year.

"Do you have a possible guess of how far away the La Guardia airport is to the JFK and how much approximately it will cost for the taxi cab fare?" the Michigan student asked the attendant awkwardly, noting that there was a large amount of time between her arrival to the La Guardia and the scheduled departure from the JFK but not sure about what more to expect.

"Oh, there is no need to worry about the distance. It is not a long ride and I would venture to guess that an average fare is roughly ten dollars. It will be fine, I'm sure!" smiled the attendant in response, apparently knowing from others experiencing like-type situations and therefore able to give this information.

I heard the news report that a terrorist leader said to be responsible for numerous attacks and tyranny was eliminated. My episodes of mental illness have been too severe for an involvement that goes beyond basic comment. I don't have a grasp on the political role that this person played in world politics enough to have sympathy or antipathy for his demise. I suppose that I could categorize him with Attila the Hun, but after reading some of the teachings of this renowned foe, I found merit in some of his philosophy that may have kept him with many supporters. I have found justice in not spending all of my savings to a zero balance simply because I don't have enough to pay all of my bills. Attila taught the Huns to not keep risking more ammunition on a battle in which they were already predicted to be defeated, instead advising that they retreat to be able to fight stronger in the next battle. I did not understand the philosophies of this terrorist leader because it was not made available to me and so I have no defense or judgment for his passing. I am not excusing Attila's reputation of being one of the most deadly of pirates in war but I can establish why he would have rapport among his warriors. He did not send them into battle to be massacred but they were guilty of many massacres on others. I don't feel that I have been educated enough to know this recent terrorist's notions on world peace because we don't understand how he could gain so much global influence without the support of **many**. What are **his** supporters saying? We never seem to hear anything about his people except for them to say that they are being forced by his regime to cooperate with these terrorist plots and certain inhumane experiments that they state are for chastisement and not exclusive to medical research. It appears that his people are taking the same position as those non-Jewish residents of Germany during the Holocaust of the 1940's.

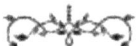

The La Guardia airport did not appear to be as large as the JFK, however it was busy enough to have a group of soliciting cab drivers waiting outside the port doors for fares, assuming that there would be ample customers for each. As soon as our Michigan traveler emerged through the port doors, an independent driver offered her space in his car. She cautiously inquired about the fare expected in consideration of the destination. To her surprise he agreed to the exact amount that the attendant had quoted, accepting her nod of approval as permission to quickly collect the largest of her carry-on bags to store on the back seat as he opened its rear door for her service.

When our Michigan student traveler boarded the overseas 747 Pan American jet at the John Fitzgerald Kennedy airport, she was surprised to see many of the other students from the University of Michigan on the same flight to Madrid for the summer program. Most of them were enrolled in the courses that she had completed on last year's visit and none of those that were enrolled in the same courses that she elected this year had been to Spain for last year's program.

CHAPTER FIFTEEN

Our Michigan traveler was excited to be en route to recapture some of the old acquaintances from last year. When the group landed in Madrid, Spain, our traveler did not catch sight of any of the others in the baggage claim area, not that anything for her could be collected there anyway. After about an hour of waiting and inquiries with the airport staff, she discovered that her luggage had been late in arriving to the John Fitzgerald Kennedy airport from the La Guardia flight and had been left behind in New York City. The staff would instruct the baggage crew to have the bags carried over on the flight leaving tomorrow and she would be able to recover them possibly in two days. Exasperated but not completely distraught, our student traveler reminded herself that she had a few articles of clothing in her large carry-on bag to use until she was able to collect the rest of her luggage. She would use the time to go to Salamanca to visit the male student admirer from the year before and expect to arrive in Seville on time for next Monday's classes, as today was Friday morning and she had the entire weekend for the necessary detour.

Her male admirer met her at the train station and she agreed to join him in his aunt's apartment for lunch during the very hot hours of the Spanish siesta that Saturday afternoon. They had an amiable discussion during the course of the meal, however, our student traveler sensed a tension among the three but guessed that it was perhaps the news that her admirer would have to leave soon after lunch to work in one of the restaurants that they had passed on foot during the walk from the train station. She had agreed to walk with him to drop him for his report for duty but would return to spend time with his aunt while he worked.

Her admirer's conversation was changed from last year and our female traveler realized the reason for it when she noticed another young woman greeting him fondly as she began to walk back to the apartment. He quickly caught up with her as she tried to jet away but he stopped her with a strong grasp around her wrist,

"Ella es una amiga… nada mas… no tiene mi corazon como tu lo tienes…! (She is a friend… nothing more… She's not like you to me…!)

"Ya lo vi! Me voy! Adios! Buena suerte! (So I've seen! I'm leaving! Good bye and good luck!)

"Por favor, intiendes que yo quiero siguir contigo! (Please, you need to understand that I want you!)

"No te creo" (I can't believe what you say!)

"Ayyy! Tengo que trabajar pero quiero que me promotes esperar para que nos hablemos cuando salgo… Por favor?! (Come on! I have to start work now but please promise that you'll wait for me… Please?!)

Our student traveler nodded in agreement but knew that she would not wait for him. She walked quickly from the restaurant back to the apartment. She knew that her former admirer's aunt had already guessed what had taken place when she answered her knock on the door of the apartment and looked into her face. Our female traveler gathered her things and made her way back to the train station. There were no words to express her disappointment. She needed to return to her adult mind quickly before she allowed romance to remove all of the possibilities of success in the already limited opportunities available to her.

"De que piensas de las solteras trabajando afuera de casa y de los puestos que se trabajan de los hombres?"

"Como?" our student traveler was so nervous that she had difficulty with the interpretation of the question.

"What do you think about women in the work force?" smiled the other male radio talk show host, quickly interceding as not to desert their guest in her moment of struggle.

"Pues… Es una buena idea, no? A mi, me gusta viajar y conocer a la gente de paises diferentes. Para crecer los amistades es para crecer la cienca para que se trabaje." (Well… it's a good objective, isn't it? I, personally like to travel and to meet people of other nations. To increase friendships is to increase the knowledge needed to do a good job)

It had been a surprise of the disc jockey in Seville to carry our female student traveler to meet with some of his friends and to request that she sing a selection of songs to be heard on the local radio station there. She was very flattered that they were generous enough to allow her non-professional expertise such an opportunity. This year the friend of the disc jockey that had been in the photograph with the female student had not re-appeared in the night club and the disc jockey had new friends.

Our female student traveler reclined in the comfortable ergonomic swivel chair, now glad that the others had continued on with the talk session without more need for comment from her. The disc jockey winked his approval at her choice of song when she had earlier been requested the impromptu selection. Her studio audience was cordial and receptive of her vocal rendition of the song but now focused on local matters and news entries. For our student traveler, it was the first time being in a radio studio but she had performed in talent shows and church services prior to this opportunity so didn't give much thought to marking this item as more than a special gift from a friend. What was more appealing to her was the news that a megastar recording artist would be arriving to perform in concert during the study program and she would be able, for the first time, to be allowed to attend his concert.

Our female traveler had never been fortunate to have been allowed to attend a top ten concert in her life and was thrilled that she would be able to join in this rare opportunity! The study group was now settled in a hostel called Hostel Europa, a family-operated and owned business that was located less than one block from the Casa de Santa Maria right off of the main *avenida.* Our female traveler often walked the long street up to the *puente* (bridge) that straddled the Rio Grande, the large and long river that extended throughout the length of the city of Seville to arrive a Las Piruetas, the *discoteca* (night club) of the disc jockey.

The medium-sized family that had proprietorship of the Hostel Europa, was very much a modern but tight-knit family. Isabel, the youngest of the children was very helpful but maintained a safe distance from the hostel guest, in that she only socialized during the special evening and weekends with the live-in community. As a family, they demonstrated the *flamenco*, a popular Spanish dance ritual before the group of traveling students when a band had been invited to play for entertainment night in the Hostel. Our female traveler was amazed by the synchronized clapping accompaniment that she clumsily attempted to join in to but did not quite make the beat with the clapping and tapping that was indeed marvelous to hear in unison. There was a tall, young woman of slender build wearing a long and colorful skirt with which she twirled and waived in time to the music as she stomped out on the hard floor the matching rhythms. Most of the dance was done with the movement of the feet, with a minimal amount of upper body movement although our female traveler would certainly not discount the dance as a vigorous chore to accomplish.

Conflict is a difficult entity of all of our lives, however, knowing the appropriate response to conflict is held by those with the education to determine where they must begin with the questions. There is a significant event that led to a series of other events which caused the breakdown of a family unit, a career and social decay. A young single mother faced her eight year old son as he ran into their townhouse apartment home one afternoon, breathless and upset with rushed words. The young mother tried to comprehend what had happened. The young lad lifted his shirt and turned around to reveal a large abrasion on his dorsal side while explaining that he and another boy child had argued and the other child opted to conclude the disagreement by striking this young mother's child with a very large stick as her son tried to escape the argument by riding away on his bicycle.

The young mother was alarmed by the news report because they had only recently moved into this subdivision of townhomes and she was suspicious of this fight taking place now, so early into their settlement there. A number of other children, some teens, were there to testify of the assault as well and instinctively, the young mother decided that she would speak to the other child's mother about the incident. The meeting was a disaster and the young mother decided to bring the local police department in for a report because the other child's mother was angered that the young mother with the injured child would suggest that her child be punished for using the large stick to hit another child.

Six months passed and another conflict arose with the young mother's male child. Because of this second conflict, the apartment management decided to terminate the lease agreements of the parents of both of the children involved in the original conflict. The young mother suffered a nervous breakdown and lost her job and all of their personal property as a result of hearing the news of her lease termination.

I have often thought on this situation and it never made logical sense until this morning. I realized that the young mother was in need of more education to be able to appropriately respond to conflict. The problem in her response occurred when her first action was to demand that the other child be physically punished for his part in the dispute. The difficult fact that needs to be first discussed should have been the events and conversation that led to the young mother's child being struck. This young mother took no responsibility for **her** own son's part in the disagreement and the apartment managers decided that parents who do not take responsibility in the wrong doings of their children will probably not keep them from destroying property and will not pay for damages that their children make and the best way to protect the interest in their establishment is to terminate those leases.

Scientific law states that there must be **two** rough surfaces rubbed together to create the resistance to create a friction in which to ignite a fire. It did not make logical sense to keep restating that the other child struck the young mother's child without first remembering that they **both** argued. The appropriate response that may have prevented the eviction should have started with the young mother cleaning her son's wounds and then questioning him about the details of the verbal discussion prior to the physical attack. Another recent review reveals that the male child that used the large stick had been prompted to do so because of the profanity that the young mother's child used during the argument and we were told that his parents were very strict in chastising their children for use of this same language. Perhaps, that child was very convinced that he must punish what he felt was very offensive as well.

CHAPTER SIXTEEN

Joining the University of Michigan group this year in Seville for their group social gatherings, were two other University students who had opted to travel the country alone as did the student from Belgium of the previous year. The two lone travelers were both female and fluent in the Spanish language, one from having been reared by parents with two separate first languages and the other having spent much time on the islands of Costa Rica.

"You really are brave to try such technical vocabulary in Spanish for not having Spanish as a first language" commented the lone traveler with the two first languages.

"What do you mean?" responded our Michigan student traveler.

"Well, my parents have different first languages, Spanish and English so that makes me have two first languages but does not give me the amount of time needed to focus on specialization in either language. We bilinguals with two first languages leave the technical words for other speakers to use primarily in their first language. It surprises me that you constantly seek to use technical words to communicate in a second language. What is even more surprising is that you get many of them right!"

"Oh…I hadn't realized I had been doing that…" answered our student traveler suddenly feeling self-conscious of her lack of dutifully memorized vocabulary words. She felt somewhat prodigal in trying to work from her English vocabulary because of convenience. She certainly wouldn't want to take similarities for granted for the small dangers that could be presented with these assumptions. An example of these small dangers is a small anecdote: Another student had been told something quite shameful by a male admirer and had responded, "Estoy embarazada!"

Instantly, the young male's expression went blank and he paused and gasped a short breath but suddenly he broke into roaring laughter.

"When will you have your baby, then…?'Embarazada' is translated 'with-child' or pregnant, not 'embarrassed'" he revealed delicately.

"Verguenza!" coached one of the elderly women who understood few words of English but somehow understood the confusion of the student.

So many strategies for adapting to the language of Spanish had been made available through the process of living the language in a native environment and reinforcements kept the students focused and less inhibited about stumbling with difficult pronunciation. They had learned very early to not feel themselves ever confident enough to tease about language…

One Saturday afternoon aboard a passenger bus headed for 'La Playa de Matalascanas' our student traveler was speaking with two young native women.

"Trabajaba en un restaurante muy elegante" said the young Spanish woman.

"Trabajaba?" involuntarily chuckled our student traveler, tickled by the way it rolled off of her own tongue. She did not often use the past imperfect form of the verb 'trabajar' and was surprised to hear it pronounced today.

"Si! Trabajaba!" responded the young Spanish woman, offended by the laughter of our student traveler, understanding it as a patronizing or belittling attitude on the part of our student traveler.

"Yo, tambien, trabaje en el restaurant de los Estados Unidos, McDonalds, hace unos anos atras," rushed on our student traveler quickly trying to remedy her outburst that was not intended to be an insult and very much wanting to repair the breach of respect.

"Pues, fue un restaurante *elegante* donde trabaje yo," insisted the young Spanish woman, still unhappy about the laughter.

It was no use to go any further, thought our student traveler, deciding to look in the opposite direction, out the window at the hills and other scenery that sped by her view as the bus made its way along the road to the popular weekend spot. She had made an enemy of the young Spanish woman but she wasn't going to keep trying to apologize because she sincerely meant no harm. Anyway, the Spanish young lady had resumed her conversation with the other native and seemed to be glad to ignore our female traveler for the remainder of the bus trip.

Shortly after the arrival to the white shores of the sea, everyone was called out of the water. For some reason, during the hottest time of the day, they did not want anyone swimming in the waters even though our traveler felt it would be the best way to remain cool. Perhaps it would be too tiring with the heat to swim or maybe it was just the time for the lifeguards to go off duty for lunch break. The beach vendors were still available and open for business during the break so our student traveler made her way to the busy beachside hut, famished because she had not yet eaten today. The entrees were very expensive and our traveler wished she had packed a lunch but found an order of smoked clams to be affordable. They were delicious, with the salt and seasoning applied close to perfection.

Another student from the group wandered up to where our student traveler sat perched upon one of the counter stools and grabbed the next stool over. She requested a sample of our student traveler's meal stating that she didn't want to buy an entire meal but did want to try something. Our student traveler quickly pushed away her greediness and offered the rest of the food to the other student. 'Maybe I can spare the calories more than she' thought our traveler as she jumped down from the stool and made her way back to the edge of the shore for a small walk. She would remember the clams as being one of the tastiest of meals that she enjoyed in Spain, however. It was a shame her good manners did not allow her to eat them all!

The Centre for International Students was an antique building explanatory of its former use as a convent during the 1800's. It had an isolated entrance lane that made it difficult to solicit because one could not feign to being 'just in the neighborhood' or 'just passing by' in order to knock on its front doors. It was located in one of the territories previously inhabited by the Muslim or Moors, Toledo, Spain- 'city of gold'. Toledo was a small municipality and looked like it could have been a biblical city such as 'Jericho' in its preservation of ancient times. It was just a small train commute to the capital, Madrid from Toledo. Now that the University of Michigan group had relocated to the Centre, the group spent even more time together because of the in-house classes.

If our student traveler had been captain of the track and field team, she could not have done a better job of sprinting across the huge acreage of the stadium floor to arrive one of the very first at the front stage for the planned concert! She had not been able to leave with the others for the train ride from Toledo to Madrid but found her way to the huge stadium where the concert for the Top ten artist and other introductory acts was to be held. She only carried a small bag that was secured by a long strap and was therefore given clearance promptly when she arrived at one of the entrances with a short line by purely good chance. Now, with not more than a handful of other fans in the entire stadium this early, she had the opportunity to pick the place of her choice of the front center standing space in front of the huge and lengthy stage.

Very soon after, our student traveler was surrounded by other fans, as she remained with her body pressed hard against the surface of the tall stage platform, pulling for her selected space as the fans that were literally packed like sardines into the standing spaces, now filled the arena. Our traveler had little opportunity to do more than stretch her neck to see what took place around her for the pressure of the other people standing with no room to even fall down in the sweltering heat. Huge tubs of water were used to douse the fans in an emergency effort to avoid more fainting as some of the fans had to be pried out of the crowd because there was no space for them to fall and they were left standing even after fainting. It was hours before the concert was scheduled to begin and many fainted fans had already been removed before the air began to cool and the effects of the tubs of water took hold.

"How about a soda?" a huge guard offered our student traveler as the student managed to grab the Pepsi can out of reach of the other fans who were reaching for it as well. She was able to take one swallow but graciously offered the rest to the others around her to duplicate her strategy of sharing as long as the contents lasted but only two or three followed her rule and much of the remainder was spilled as too many hands struggled for the next sip.

"Where are you from?" questioned a spokesperson from one of the news reporting crews that had arrived to cover the event, choosing our student traveler who was conversing with the English-speaking guard because she was one of the few English speakers on the front stage area that was also speaking to the Spanish guests.

They apparently wanted someone to translate to the Spanish natives as well as answer questions in English.

"I'm a student of the University of Michigan, located in Ann Arbor, Michigan and I'm studying with other students here for the study abroad program!" explained our student traveler.

"What do you want to say about the performer that you're about to see?" questioned the spokesperson of the news crew to one of the Spanish natives.

When the other young lady hesitated to answer, not understanding, our student traveler jumped in "Que quieres decir del cantante que viene?"

"A mi, me gusta a el. Es una maravilla esta persona. Ahhh-ayyyyy!" responded the Spanish young lady losing herself in a loud scream.

"She says that he's one of the best and she really likes his songs. She's very happy to be here!" translated our student traveler for the confused look of the television spokesperson.

In response to her voluntary translation duties, the guard, who turned out to be a personal employee of the Top ten performer, awarded our student traveler with a backstage passage authorization to be used when the concert performances were concluded.

Our student traveler was instructed to board the passenger tour bus of the performing crew while the guard of the Top ten performer finished up at the concert site. The Michigan student sat quietly listening to the background singers croon unlike anything she had heard so close by and she marveled at their talent, understanding that quite a bit of training must be acquired to even be a backup performer. She only thought of possibly catching a glimpse of the Top ten performer so that he would know that she existed and was there from his homeland to support his work. The guard finally boarded the tour bus and sat beside our female traveler and he told her that she would be joining the group for a pool party at the hotel. Our student traveler was a little disappointed that there was no mention of the Top ten performer being part of the party but did not show it in her smile of agreement to spend time with the performing crew.

As it turned out, the crew decided to cancel the pool party and retire to their own accommodations as it was now the very early morning hours of the following day. The guard invited the young lady back to his suite for a room service pizza and to show her some of his portfolio as a substitute for the pool party. Our student traveler looked on with guarded interest at the magazine articles and photographs that contained some of the experiences of the guard in his employment for various Top ten performers. Afterwards, our student traveler was allowed to sleep in one of the armchairs until dawn the next morning so that she could travel to the student lodgings in Toledo when the train service was again available. Years later, when the video collection of the tour aired, our student traveler discovered that her personage had been caught on film the night of the concert, smiling in the midst of the huge crowd of fans. Perhaps it was fate and travel or perhaps the brief snapshot was chosen on purpose. But for whatever reason it showed up, it is there!

The Michigan student was very much grateful for having been given the opportunity to experience such a unique privilege but was glad that she could return to her ordinary life, content that those experiencing careers of fame were well equipped to well serve the masses of loving fans. Although we hear of the passing of worldwide influences, they remain incorporated in the world that continues to survive. We must anticipate that our metamorphoses will happen eventually as well but our endeavor is always to leave a remnant of our existence to sustain the growth of the generations beyond us. The University of Michigan student traveler provides not only her adventure but the knowledge that we do not make our journeys alone. There are many ingredients that create an endless dichotomy of expectations that come to be as a result of the existence of independent thought and independent choice. Perhaps, we are regretful in our decisions of the past. However, every experience must have its place as a lesson learned as a result of life. The University of Michigan student did not choose to condense responsibility to a mere 'just find a job that pays the bills' but chose to pursue an avenue that previously did not include many of her predecessors. Change is a much coveted rite but with change comes the risk of much suffering, much disappointment, some discomfort and possible elimination. Maybe we'll choose to hope for the dreams, realize the change and somehow manage to pay our expenses but if we do so, I sincerely hope that it is with the passion, creativity, generosity and integrity of this same student.

Away rolled the train into the night and although the Michigan student had not yet exited the Spanish border, it was farewell to this country and its people for now.

CHAPTER SEVENTEEN

HELP WANTED

For immediate hire, I need someone to do my thinking for me. They must possess the qualities to get other people to take the blame for the things that happen when they are around. Applicants must be able to do without sleep and food at any given moment. Position must be filled because I do have to think about death and I have so many things that people do not want me to have that it seems useless to keep trying to protect them. Please contact that female who was born in South Haven Community Hospital on February 5, 1967. Those willing to be able to imagine a salary will be given priority for an interview. My documentation and accreditations will not be necessary to replicate because we haven't been able to convince people that they are genuine, anyway.

We would like to hear from YOU!

"I sure am glad that we have a new way to get our payments here faster! Now... all we have to do is solve the problem of convincing our customers to use it..." groaned the Customer Service supervisor.

"Yeah... I know what you mean! I don't know how appealing it is to leave my home and pay an extra ten dollars and fifty cents to get my payment credited to my account just because a representative is calling me to demand it..." agreed the Branch Manager.

"Well, they may understand when they are twenty-nine days past due that making that investment to keep the account from being over thirty days delinquent will keep their credit from being negatively affected and be convinced by that to use the service," offered the Branch Operations Manager.

"Some of them have been late so many times that another payment reported over thirty days past due is not going to matter to them!" countered the Branch Manager.

"Why does the company want us to use this wire pay method? That contract costs a lot of money!" remarked the Customer Service Supervisor.

"Well our Customer service losses have been very, very high and it's because of the delinquency ratio. We need new ways to keep it at an acceptable level. You heard the Western Union representative. The money is here within just minutes and we don't have to wait for the lockbox to report the payment the next day to see if it has arrived. We get a report just seconds after they push the 'send' button from the payment location," answered the Branch Operations manager.

"What do you think?" the Customer Service supervisor prompted the Customer Service Representative Senior who had been sitting quietly listening but inspecting the form that had been used during the demonstration. The Customer Service supervisor leaned back with crossed legs and folded his arms across his chest as he and the others waited for a reply.

"Let's see...Maybe expecting the customers to agree to payment just because the service is now available is unlikely, however, I think the representatives can convince them to wire their payments if they, themselves are convinced that they have to have them use it. Sometimes new services go left unused because they are too complicated to teach to the customers," commented the Customer Service representative senior.

"I agree! I think we should start by making a big push for the representatives to push the service here in the office instead of leaving it to the advertisement that the company has paid to have sent to the customers to do the job alone" joined the Branch Manager.

"One great thing that we have to offer is the low rate in comparison to the standard fee for wiring money! They can sell it that way, for one… What else?" added the Branch Operations manager, thinking aloud.

"You've been looking at that form. Why?" questioned the Customer Service supervisor of the Customer Service representative senior.

"I thought if we could each have a sample copy completed beside the phone of each representative, it may help them to explain the process so that the customers aren't confused when they get to the payment location... even if they are unsure of what to do when they arrive, perhaps they can be instructed to take the 800 number with them to the payment location so that they can be helped 'step-by-step' through the payment process if necessary" replied the Customer Service representative senior.

"Hey-y! How about we hang up posters around the office? Having some type of visuals on the walls may help too!" suggested the Branch manager, now beginning to get excited about the campaign.

"I have a lot more performance reviews to get done... How are you with your workload this week?" asked the Customer Service supervisor of the Customer service representative senior.

"Oh, I'll work something out! I'll get started on the samples for the representatives and see if I can come up with a slogan for a poster that'll get them excited about pushing for wire payments!" helpfully agreed the Customer Service representative senior.

"Well, you know that you have a representative B that has an Art degree, right? He might be willing to help if you think it's necessary..." suggested the Customer Service supervisor.

"Very good, then! I'll get started!" ended the Customer service representative senior, as she had her instruction and pulling herself up to stand, ready to get back to her work station.

"Shall we take the money for the supplies from Petty cash or do we need an expense report?" asked the Customer Service supervisor.

"We need to use Branch income and we'll have to use an expense report to support it. Let us know when you need to have the check written and I'll get the Administrative supervisor to have one of her clerks prepare it!" answered the Branch Manager nodding in the direction of the Customer Service representative senior.

As it turned out, the Customer Service representative senior did not have to approach representative B with the Art degree for his help. During his lunch break the next day, he wandered over to her work station.

"They said that you may need some help with posters, perhaps?" the representative B with the Art degree inquired.

"Well, yes! I see they've already informed you. I did come up with a small sketch of what I would like… Let's have a look!" smiled the Customer Service representative senior, as she welcomed representative B with the art degree to come closer to show him something. She pulled a small sheet of paper from her paper tray and laid it flat on the desk surface.

"Here's what I want:" started the Customer Service representative senior, as she pointed at the lines of the 'stick-like' figure scrawled on the paper holding up a stack of currency bills. The slogan atop read 'Don't overburden your cashier! Use Western Union Quick Collect!'.

"You see, there's supposed to be the cashier and she is struggling to hold up this *huge* stack of money! I want the slogan to read: 'Don't overburden your cashier! Use Western Union Quick Collect!'. Can you see what I need?" probed the Customer Service representative senior of representative B with the Art degree.

"Yeah, oh, yeah! I can work with this..." asserted the representative B with the Art degree taking the paper with the sketch in hand, delicately.

"Are you going to do some art work for us? I know you'll do a fine job! That's your specialty isn't it...?.." commented representative A who was walking by the work station of the Customer Service representative senior and overheard the talk concerning the campaign project. She had quickly scanned the paper to know what the two others were planning as she stood beside representative B with the Art degree.

"We'll see how it turns out... I'll do what I can!" shyly accepted the representative B with the Art degree.

"Oh, my! How wonderful! This is exactly what I wanted and even more!" the Customer Service representative senior commented as she stood gazing in awe at the finished demonstration of the project. Representative B with the Art degree had so well personified the struggle of the cashier with pretty pearl beads around her neck and heeled pumps, with an exasperated look for a facial expression struggling to lift the stack of currency bills.

The other representatives all stood and leaned in close to eye the completed work. There were giggles and 'oohs' all around as they all surveyed the poster.

"I think we're going to have to frame this! I'm going to take it to the 'Big Guys' so they can have a look at it!" the Customer Service supervisor walked through the crowd of spectators and picked up the poster.

The Customer Service representative senior and the representatives all returned to their work stations as the

Customer Service supervisor crossed the aisle of work stations to the office of the Branch Manager and beckoned the Branch Operations manager to join them in that office.

The Customer Service supervisor returned without the poster and commented to the Customer Service representative senior and the representative B with the Art degree that the Branch Manager requested to keep the poster for now and would see to them later.

"It doesn't seem like that machine has gone an entire ten minutes without printing a payment report! I'm really surprised to see that the customers' responses to the representatives' push has come through for us!" noted the Customer Service supervisor, taking the responsibility to personally pull the Western Union payment receipts off of the printer to distribute to the representatives as he walked around to the work stations to survey the content of the conversations during the 'prime-time' calling hours.

"I agree with you! I'm very pleased with the response!" remarked the Customer Service representative senior, glancing at the poster which now hung on the wall next to her work station on the expensive mount and frame that the Branch management had seen to providing for its debut.

They all seem to be now in the habit of priming themselves to request wire payments by looking at the poster before dialing the customer contact numbers to reinforce the campaign strategies. The Customer Service representative senior was even glad to see that American Express would be soon presenting their similar package in a short time that could be used as an alternative. There would be a few adjustments to make to accommodate the additional equipment, however, they would have to try to make use of the paid-for contract for this new vendor as well so that the company would not lose the benefit of this Western Union competitor. It is not wise to allow a complete monopoly on a vital collection remedy to one company from a corporate viewpoint. It was understood that although the customers had already been trained to use the Western Union package, the American Express option came with a slightly lower rate that could be considered if they went to a payment location that offered both. As it was, the payment process was predicted to be very similar to the Western Union wire pay so there would not be much that they would have to reteach except the difference in forms and 'code' words.

The campaign was a success! Proof of the efforts of the representatives had been demonstrated in the delinquency reports and credit losses had been decreased. The Customer Service representative senior was glad to have been part of the implementation of a strategy that proved effective but was most pleased for the communication that arrived intact to the mind of the representative B with the Art degree from her simple sketch and slogan. Representative B was successful in his promotion to representative A with this work as a consideration as well as his other work plan items.

The Customer Service representative senior thought back to her interview for a position in this office and a response that she gave when the Branch Manager had remarked that they had a very small customer base that would accommodate her Spanish translator specialization,

"It is better to have an option that you don't need than to need an option that you do not have. I have found in the past that after I begin with few customers that need the availability of a Spanish speaker, that eventually the need does become real"

In this illustration, we found that the business of customer provisions does not exclude the internal customer base. It was a great threshold to enter for the acceptance of the entire part of the society that the Morrocan mentioned was the success of his people. Miles and miles can separate the ethnicity and cultures of the human element, however, we have now established evidence of a commonality in making use of the value of the components within each.

CHAPTER EIGHTEEN

Fresh air! The days have been very hot and humid making the effort to take walks and get exercise more a strong discipline than a preference. I would like to get my botany studies into my summer schedule; however, it will be a tight fit! I have now begun to realize that my accomplishments are going to have to graduate from the 'success once it's on paper' approach to the 'I know what I have to accomplish and stop waiting for a show of approval' approach to get my assignments completed. Thinking about getting things accomplished is best motivated by another anecdote that explains about a mother and wife who battled within herself to make something happen when she, herself was not really convinced that she wanted the change to occur.

"Honey, you don't understand! Mom just needs to smoke sometimes. I have so-o many responsibilities and I need to be able to do just this one bad thing…"

'He's always been my moral support and now he seems so discouraged about my smoking habit!' thought the young mother. She felt self-conscious now that he frequently requested that she quit the habit. He was now a pre-teen and she had been a smoker since he was only three years old. It had not been a debatable subject before now.

"I-I just want my mom to be a healthy mom...!" pleadingly coaxed her son.

She knew that the school officials had been coaching the child on how to approach smoking parents and she resented that they didn't understand the pressures that she experienced in trying to support her family. She already had so little reward in her life; how could they deny her this one thing?

"Do you remember when we lived in Indiana and you were looking all over for your cigarettes?" questioned her son slowly.

"Yes..."

"Well...I took them and I broke them all up in the back yard because I hated them!"

"I'm sorry... I didn't know it was you... I'm sorry!"

"I just wanted you to know that I did that..." ended her son as he finally exited the room to leave her privately to smoke the cigarette that she had removed from the package before he entered.

She had made a compromise by not smoking in their presence now. She didn't want to witness their disgusted looks when she did the terrible thing...

It was a while before she could brush away this flag of guilt. Eventually the next day, she did smoke again but the impact of these confrontations was getting stronger and stronger. It seemed now that the only time that she could be allowed to enjoy a cigarette without guilt was after she had cleaned the house to immaculacy or when they were away spending the night with other family members or friends.

This struggling mother had always felt that children are allies for parents and knew that this time she was asking for more understanding than they were willing to allow.

"You know, smoking doesn't really help people lose weight, Mom!" scolded her daughter, the eldest of the two children, walking up to the automobile as her mother had arrived home and parked the car but was finishing a cigarette before rising out from the car. She was a little more subtle than her younger brother but it still was evident that the school officials had included her in the anti-smoking campaign as well. She had, it seemed, left a pamphlet on the dining room table with advice on how to leave the habit intentionally for her mother.

"Sweetie, Mom is trying very hard to smoke just a little but I don't like the pressure of everyone pressuring me to quit…!" remarked the struggling Mom, hurt by another attack.

"What do you mean?! …What are you talking about?!!"

"You keep bringing this literature and that brochure and books home, all about my smoking habit! I'm really getting frustrated because I am very aware that everyone wants me to quit but I don't like to be nagged about it!"

"…about YOU??!! That is for ME! My counselors thought I started smoking!" indignantly retorted the daughter of the struggling mother.

The struggling mother was embarrassed that she had been so irritable and defensive.

"I apologize for my behavior… I know that people just want to be helpful. *Have* you started smoking?" she delicately inquired.

"No!"

The struggling mother was glad to know that her poor behavior had not so far influenced her children into the same habit but knew that it could not be expected for them to go unaffected. She suspected that some of their juvenile stunts were influenced by her poor choices and she wondered if they were far from the norm.

"If you can't quit, you can't quit..." offered her daughter, perhaps frustrated as much as her mother.

"Maybe I'll try harder..."

"It's up to *you*!

Although the struggling mother could attribute most of the tension she felt with her children to their stage of development and the transition into independent thought, there remained others, specifically her husband, that tolerated the habit but would approach the subject too, when it appeared excessive.

"Mi Amor! ...Otro cigarro??!! Ojala que un dia tu dejes de este vicio!" he started into this accusation that he seemed to be using as a crutch by making it the culprit for all of their disagreements as much as for why she was used the cigarettes.

"Tu bien sabes que yo pago por mis propios cigarros! Solo quieres pelear conmigo! Por que?" objected the struggling mother. She couldn't understand why her husband objected to the habit when she never asked for him to use his earnings to buy them for her. Like her daughter said, the habit did not help people lose weight; however, this mom noticed that she had less of an appetite when she supplemented her intake with cigarettes.

"I can't do this anymore!" the struggling mother thought to herself. "It's just not right! ...It's not right! I am an adult! I want to smoke and I can't!! "

It was true. She would have to quit. Not because she wanted to quit but because everyone in the world around her would not allow her to smoke anymore. She was not allowed to say that there was so much air pollution that it didn't matter what happened to her lungs. She was not allowed to say that she knew others who smoked for years and were not affected. She was not allowed to say that it was the only thing that she had to look forward to. She was not allowed to say that she needed to smoke to relax. She was not allowed to say that she had terrible dreams when she did not smoke. She was not allowed to say that her life was not worth saving. She was not allowed to say that she only used the money that would have been used to over eat on cigarettes. She was not allowed to say that it was alright so long as she smoked in a room alone. She was not allowed to say that it had only become a habit at nearly thirty years of age... For once, just today, she would allow them to force her to quit the habit!

"They'll all know what they have caused...They'll realize that I really, really need to smoke. Maybe they'll be ashamed..." she quietly vowed angrily, feeling the humility of a chastened child instead of the middle aged woman that she could see in the medicine chest mirror of the bathroom.

She not only got through that day, she got through the following day and the days after until she accomplished a week... "Don't open the box!" she mumbled to herself...where had she heard that? She started without the intention of disposing of the package of cigarettes. She planned that eventually she would get back to those cigarettes- it just wasn't going to be this day. 'I know I can be better than their manipulation. I want them to learn to allow me to make my own choices. They need to understand that they can't keep treating me like this!' Soon the week became two weeks and then three and finally one month. She knew that it would be many months before she would stop experiencing the involuntary phantom 'pulls' of nicotine. She had been successful at least two times during the years of smoking to stop for more than five months each time but she was not planning to quit like that this time.

"I just won't smoke today, that's all..." the struggling mother kept telling herself. For once, her tendency to procrastinate helped her in a positive way and she justified another day of not smoking as much as she did when she delayed in leaving the habit.

The most amazing thing about her new strategy is that it was a pact made with herself. She didn't want anyone to know that she had not smoked recently and was fortunate that no one commented about it. The struggling mother knew of others who announced their victory of quitting only to, shortly after, start the habit all over again. The tragedies and disappointments that she had used as cues to smoke, no longer prompted the involuntary craving for the vice of cigarettes.

The struggling mother had reached nearly seven months without interruption before anyone commented on the change.

The accomplishment was proudly announced by the husband of the struggling mother to one of his in-laws. His wife's only response was to smile and change the subject.

She did not like to discuss the habit with her family or anyone else's family.

The most rewarding benefit of her endeavor is that she was free from the guilt that it was her fault when things went wrong. She did not have to come up with excuses to leave the room so that she could have a cigarette. She noticed the surprise in her mother's face when she could spend the entire day helping her with chores in her house without making an excuse to go for a walk. She could make long trips out of town with her newest child and not have to pull at a rest area to have a cigarette. She didn't have to look nervously around to see who was looking at her to catch her taking a 'pull'. She did not have to lie about the reason she showed up late for appointments. She could work straight through assignments and get more done in a short period of time. She no longer had to think about people catching a whiff of the aroma of smoke on her clothing. She no longer had to worry about planning to go to the beach so that she could hide behind the foliage to privately smoke. The extra money was much needed now for the new baby, especially for diapers.

It was a small miracle that she had been able to get pregnant after all of the years with just the two children. The struggling mother, over forty, was in remarkably good health and now she worried less about over exertion on her cardiovascular system without cigarette smoking factored into her lifestyle. She had always known that smokers often lose the benefit of taste of the food entrees that they are served however what she did not realize was that once she returned to non-smoker that she would taste the true richness of the seasonings and be more quickly satisfied. Her brain now accepted that she had eaten even after one serving and would not allow her to go to a second serving, noting that she was no longer hungry.

"Well, I guess remembering that I had happiness before I began the smoking habit will help me accept that I will never return to it."Eighteen months after her last smoked cigarette she removed a new package of cigarettes from the door compartment of her car. She had purchased it when she had reached six months of abstinence but kept it there. "Do not open the box!" Where had she heard that?! She had heard that others were able to smoke on special occasions after quitting the habit but she would not risk losing the amount of dedication that it took to get to this eighteen months of abstinence.

"I'm a smoke-aholic! I can't have just one...!" the struggling mother finally opened the box of the cigarettes purchased one year ago. One by one she removed them, breaking them into at least ten parts each.

"Now they can tell everyone that I was tricked into using cigarettes after eighteen months of quitting. I don't want to fight anymore, if they don't want to know the truth!"

The habit was no longer part of the struggling mother's life but its absence did not conclude the tragedies and disappointments that continued to happen.She continued to have disagreements with her children and husband and other family members on occasion. She continued to feel that others could be severe in their scrutiny of her morals. She continued to know that there were other areas of her life that could be improved. She continued to be accused of things that she objected to being involved in. She continued to find things to laugh about. She continued to make others laugh. She continued with her gift of remaining calm in traumatic situations. She continued to be late for appointments. She continued to come up with clever things to do and say. She continued to be inspired by fear. The only difference was that the guilt of being blamed for smoking was no longer hers.

She remembered when she rented the house in Indiana and what the owner had once remarked, "Maybe you can believe that you want to live here… Here's some of your rent money so that you can buy some flowers for the beds in front of the house!"

"Maybe I can believe that I want to live here… Maybe it can be good right where I am. Maybe I need to stop planning to abuse my body today to get to a better body tomorrow. Maybe I can relax in the bathtub just the same as a thin woman. Maybe I can lotion and perfume my body just the same as a thin woman… This is my body today and it likes to make itself take long walks when I don't feel like it. It pushes itself to make another trip up the stairs when I don't feel like it. It pushes itself to grab my sleeping child from the back seat of the car when I go into the grocery store, or into my relatives' homes even when I don't feel like it… Maybe I can return to enjoying my life again" agreed the struggling mother.

Perhaps, this is the real change that needed to happen. Maybe I can agree to leave things in my life just as they are… maybe they can be left just as they are!

CHAPTER NINETEEN

This has been a book of juxtapositions! You see, I was that substitute teacher! I was that female citizen. I was that University of Michigan student. I was that young mother who was evicted. I was that Customer Service representative senior. And I was the struggling mother and wife who eventually decided to quit the habit of cigarette smoking just because others refused to allow me to do it.

Maybe what was worthwhile to say is that we may all be judged differently and we can continue to find the fault in others each time we are accused of doing what is bad. What I have discovered, now, is that it only delays the acceptance of a reality that makes sense when we refuse to claim responsibility for the things that we are told are inaccurate. If it is bad to someone, it can be judged bad. My societies without judgment leave me without police protection, without homes for my children, without emergency workers who can administer cardiopulmonary resuscitation and no reasonable advice to pass on to my students. Can we find peace in this perceived world? Let's review in each story the strategies of communication that were vital but not the norm of conventional thought. Some philosophies are not easily translated into different societies and when there is an attempt to incorporate an acceptable practice for one society into another it can become a blatant misinterpretation of good intention.

Let me simply say that my life since the inception of this novel analysis has evolved from the restraint of uselessness to the realm of expectation. The prompts are difficult to locate each day but I awake with a mission that must be completed before I sleep. Years from now, if I have not reached my metamorphoses, I know that I'll return to these stories that endeared our hearts to what is good and what is pleasant to dwell upon. *Thanks for everything!*

...Thanks for everything...

The End

www.ingramcontent.com/pod-product-compliance
Lightning Source LLC
LaVergne TN
LVHW050024080526
838202LV00069B/6901